WALCH PUBLISHING

16 Extraordinary American Women

Second Edition

D0863998

**Emma
Hahn**

Photo Credits

Elizabeth Cochrane Seaman	© 1967 Dover Publications
Ka'iulani	© 1995 Courtesy of Hawaii State Archives
Eleanor Roosevelt	© 1995 Courtesy of Franklin D. Roosevelt Library
Georgia O'Keeffe	© 1931 UPI/BETTMAN
Dorothea Lange	© 1995 the Dorothea Lange Collection, The Oakland Museum of California, the City of Oakland. Gift of Paul S. Taylor.
Rachel Carson	Photo courtesy of Social and Public Art Resource Center
Ella Fitzgerald	© 1995 AP/WIDE WORLD PHOTOS
Rosalyn Sussman Yalow	© 1977 UPI/BETTMAN
Nikki Giovanni	© 1995 Elizabeth Isele
Donna Karan	© 1993 Malcolm Clarke/AP/WIDE WORLD PHOTOS
Bonnie Blair	© 1994 Dylan Martinez/REUTERS/BETTMAN
Eileen Collins	© 2003 AP/WIDE WORLD PHOTOS
Ruth Bader Ginsburg	© 1995 AP/WIDE WORLD PHOTOS
Susan Butcher	© 2006 AP/WIDE WORLD PHOTOS
Nancy Pelosi	© 2007 AP/WIDE WORLD PHOTOS

2   3   4   5   6   7   8   9   10

ISBN 978-0-8251-6279-4

Copyright © 1996, 2008

J. Weston Walch, Publisher

P. O. Box 658 · Portland, Maine 04104-0658

www.walch.com

Printed in the United States of America

Contents

To the Teacher

According to *Reading Next: A Vision for Action and Research in Middle and High School Literacy,* a report to the Carnegie Corporation of New York (2004, second edition), "High-interest, low-difficulty texts play a significant role in an adolescent literacy program and are critical for fostering the reading skills of struggling readers and the engagement of all students. In addition to using appropriate grade-level textbooks that may already be available in the classroom, it is crucial to have a range of texts in the classroom that link to multiple ability levels and connect to students' background experiences."

Biographies about extraordinary people are examples of one such kind of text. The 16 Americans described in this collection should both inspire and reassure students. As students read, your instruction can include approaches that will support not only comprehension, but also learning from passages.

Reading and language arts skills not only enrich students' academic lives but also their personal lives. The *Extraordinary Americans* series was written to help students gain confidence as readers. The biographies were written to pique students' interest while engaging their understanding of vocabulary, recalling facts, identifying the main idea, drawing conclusions, and applying knowledge. The added value of reading these biographies is that students will learn about other people and, perhaps, about themselves.

Students will read stories demonstrating that great things are accomplished by everyday people who may have grown up just like them—or maybe even with greater obstacles to overcome. Students will discover that being open to new ideas, working hard, and believing in one's self make them extraordinary people, too!

Structure of the Book

The Biographies

The collection of stories can be used in many different ways. You may assign passages for independent reading or engage students in choral reading. No matter which strategies you use, each passage contains pages to guide your instruction.

At the end of each passage, you will find a series of questions. The questions are categorized, and you can assign as many as you wish. The purposes of the questions vary:

- **Remembering the Facts:** Questions in this section engage students in a direct comprehension strategy, and require them to recall and find information while keeping track of their own understanding.

- **Understanding the Story:** Questions posed in this section require a higher level of thinking. Students are asked to draw conclusions and make inferences.

- **Getting the Main Idea:** Once again, students are able to stretch their thinking. Questions in this section are fodder for dialog and discussion around the extraordinary individuals and an important point in their lives.

- **Applying What You've Learned:** Proficient readers internalize and use the knowledge that they gain after reading. The question or activity posed allows for students to connect what they have read to their own lives.

In the latter part of the book, there are additional resources to support your instruction.

Vocabulary

A list of key words is included for each biography. The lists can be used in many ways. Assign words for students to define, use them for spelling lessons, and so forth.

Answer Key

An answer key is provided. Responses will likely vary for Getting the Main Idea and Applying What You've Learned questions.

Additional Activities

Extend and enhance students' learning! These suggestions include conducting research, creating visual art, exploring cross-curricular activities, and more.

References

Learn more about each extraordinary person or assign students to discover more on their own. Start with the sources provided.

To the Student

"...Remember the Ladies, and be more generous and favorable to them than your ancestors. Do not put such unlimited power into the hands of the Husbands.... If particular care and attention is not paid to the Ladies, we are determined to foment a Rebellion, and will not hold ourselves bound by any Laws in which we have no voice, or Representation."

—Abigail Adams, 1776

Many women have made a great difference in American history. The ways in which they lived their lives have brought positive changes for all Americans. This book contains the stories of 16 women from diverse economic, ethnic, racial, social, and geographic backgrounds. They are judges, writers, artists, astronauts, musicians, scientists, sportswomen, politicians, and businesswomen. Some of their voices you may know; others you may have never heard. Each has made an extraordinary contribution to America's heritage and to our lives today.

The 16 American women included in this book are:

- Elizabeth Cochrane Seaman (Nellie Bly), a journalist who uncovered social injustices

- Mary Jane Colter, an architect who designed buildings in the Southwest

- Ka'iulani, a Hawaiian princess who fought to keep Hawaii as an independent nation

- Eleanor Roosevelt, a humanitarian and distinguished First Lady

- Georgia O'Keeffe, an artist who painted beautiful flowers, bones, mountains, and clouds

- Dorothea Lange, a photojournalist who took portraits of people in real life

- Rachel Carson, a conservationist who fought to control the use of pesticides

- Ella Fitzgerald, a Grammy-winning singer who became America's "First Lady of Jazz"

- Rosalyn Sussman Yalow, a Nobel Prize-winning doctor who developed a test to help detect disease

- Nikki Giovanni, a poet who gave back to her community

- Donna Karan, a fashion designer who made clothing to help women feel better about themselves

- Bonnie Blair, an Olympic speed skater who has set several records

- Eileen Collins, an astronaut who became the first woman to command a space shuttle

- Ruth Bader Ginsburg, only the second woman to become a Supreme Court Justice

- Susan Butcher, a dogsled racer who won the Iditarod four times

- Nancy Pelosi, who became the first woman Speaker of the House

I hope you will enjoy reading the stories of these amazing women. As you read about each woman's experience, you may be able to imagine ways in which you, too, can make a difference.

—Emma Hahn

Elizabeth Cochrane Seaman (Nellie Bly)

Journalist

Elizabeth Cochrane was born in 1864 in Cochran's Mills, Pennsylvania. The town was named after her father, Michael Cochran. Elizabeth added the "e" to her last name to make her name more elegant.

Other mothers in the town dressed their daughters in practical shades of gray and brown. But Elizabeth's mother chose bright pink outfits for her daughter. So Elizabeth was called "Pink."

Elizabeth grew up with nine brothers and sisters. She went to the public school down the street. Her father died when she was only six years old. Her mother soon remarried. But the marriage ended in divorce—something very unusual in those days.

Elizabeth went to college to become a teacher. But she had to drop out after her first year. She could not pay the tuition.

Elizabeth got her first taste of journalism at the age of 18. She moved to Pittsburgh to live with her mother after leaving college. In 1885, the *Pittsburgh Dispatch* published an editorial called "What Girls Are Good For." The article was against women's suffrage. It criticized women having lives outside their homes. Elizabeth was outraged. She wrote an anonymous letter to the editor of the paper. She signed it "The Lonely Orphan Girl." She provided no return address.

The editor was so curious that he placed an ad in his paper to find Elizabeth. "If the 'Lonely Orphan Girl' will send her name and address to this office … she will confer a favor and receive the information she desires."

The next day, Elizabeth went to the editor's office. He asked her to write a response to the column, and she did. Her article, "The Girl Puzzle," was published on the first page of the Sunday paper. It defended working women in Pittsburgh. It was a big hit. Soon Elizabeth became a regular reporter for the *Pittsburgh Dispatch.*

Back then, writing for a newspaper was not considered "ladylike." So women reporters signed their columns with a pseudonym (a made-up name). Elizabeth wrote under the name Nellie Bly. "Nellie Bly" was a popular song written years before.

Nellie did not just write about women's suffrage. She also reported on poor working conditions in local factories. She wrote about the problems working women faced. She wrote about slums. She even wrote about divorce.

The *Dispatch* soon sent Nellie to Mexico. She was to write about the difference between the lives of the very rich and the very poor. She also wrote about Mexican politics. Nellie's articles were so powerful that the Mexican government finally made her leave. Her writing was later published in a book called *Sixth Months in Mexico.*

In 1887, Nellie returned to the United States. She went to Joseph Pulitzer's paper, *New York World,* in New York City. She convinced Pulitzer to let her report on the cruelty and neglect suffered by mentally ill patients. Nellie wanted her report to be accurate. So she acted insane. She was admitted to the Women's Lunatic Asylum on Blackwell's Island. Nellie spent ten days inside the asylum. Her reports shocked the world. They helped to change the care for the mentally ill.

From then on, Nellie wore many different disguises. She was one of the first undercover reporters. She worked in a sweatshop. She had herself arrested to see what happened to women in jail. She danced in a corps de ballet. When something seemed unfair, she jumped right in to investigate. Then she revealed the problem in print.

Pulitzer was so pleased with Nellie's success that he gave her a new challenge. She was to take a trip around the world. There was one catch.

She had to try to beat the record set in the novel, *Around the World in Eighty Days*. Nellie made the journey in 72 days, 6 hours, and 11 minutes. She traveled by boat, train, wagon, and horse—even a rickshaw.

Nellie's luggage was just one bag, only 16 inches long and 7 inches tall! She was determined to travel light. People thought a woman would be held back by all of the luggage she would require. The newspaper printed daily accounts of her trip on its front page. Nellie Bly became a worldwide sensation. It was the highlight of her career.

In 1895, Nellie was on a train to New York from the Midwest. She met a wealthy businessman named Robert Seaman on the train. They were married a few days later. He was 72; Nellie was 28. Robert only lived for ten more years.

After Robert's death, Nellie took over his companies. She improved conditions for workers. Then Nellie retired from business and went to Europe. She sent letters back to the *New York World* about the problems there. Those problems led to World War I. After the war, Nellie returned to the United States. She had a new job at the *New York Evening Journal*.

Nellie Bly is most often remembered for her trip around the world. But she was also one of the first reporters to write about the unfairness in this world.

Nellie had proven herself in the male world of journalism. At first, her readers only focused on the fact that she was a woman. But Nellie turned that attention toward important issues. Her stories sold papers. They boosted public awareness of social problems.

At the time of her death in 1922, the *New York Evening Journal* wrote, "Nellie Bly was the best reporter in America."

Remembering the Facts

1. What was Nellie Bly's real name?

2. Why did Nellie want to go to college?

3. What was the name of the first newspaper Nellie wrote for?

4. Where did Nellie's pseudonym come from?

5. Name three topics that Nellie Bly wrote about.

6. How did Nellie get the information for her report on the mentally ill?

7. What was the highlight of Nellie's career?

8. What did Nellie do when she was in Europe?

Understanding the Story

9. Nellie took the time to write about many problems in the world. Do you think, as some people did, that she did it only to draw attention to herself?

10. At one time, Nellie wanted to become a teacher. Do you think she taught through her writing?

Getting the Main Idea

Why do you think Nellie Bly is a good role model for young people today?

Applying What You've Learned

If you saw a situation in which people were being treated unfairly, how would you try to correct it?

Mary Jane Colter

Architect

Mary Jane Colter was one of America's most talented and creative architects. But she is also one of the least known. Eleven of the buildings she designed are in the National Register of Historic Places. Mary was a woman working in a male-dominated field. Male architects such as Frank Lloyd Wright are more well known.

Mary was born in 1869 in Pittsburgh, Pennsylvania. The Civil War was over. During her childhood, Mary's family often moved. They lived in Texas, Colorado, and Minnesota. Much of this territory was newly settled. Texas and Minnesota were new states. And Colorado did not become a state until 1876.

Mary was 18 when her father died. Her mother decided the family would stay in St. Paul, Minnesota.

Mary had always wanted to be an artist. She was inspired by images she remembered from the American West. She did not know then that they would become the focus of her life's work.

Mary convinced her mother to let her go to the California School of Design in San Francisco. She promised that she would learn valuable skills. These, she said, would help her earn money to help support her mother and sister.

While in school, Mary was an apprentice to an architect. The job helped her pay for classes. She was fascinated by the new theories of architecture. They suggested that new buildings should maintain the look of their natural and historic environment. People had long thought that America's buildings should be designed in the old, European fashion. This style had little in common with the new and expanding United States.

Mary got her degree when she was 23. She returned to St. Paul. She found a job teaching drawing. As promised, she was earning money to help support her family. However, she never gave up her love of the West. So she applied for a job with the Fred Harvey Company.

Fred Harvey was building several hotels and restaurants. As the railroads expanded across the country, he knew that travelers would need places to rest and eat. He became famous for his first-class hotels and service.

Harvey wanted his guests to experience the "real" West. In 1902, he hired Mary to decorate an "Indian Building." It was built next to his new Alvarado Hotel in Albuquerque, New Mexico. It was supposed to just be a summer job. But Harvey loved Mary's work so much that he continued to work with her for the next 46 years.

In time, she became his chief architect and designer. He built a number of buildings on the southern rim of the Grand Canyon. Mary designed and oversaw the construction of all of them.

Mary's first project was Hopi House in 1904. She had always loved Native American architecture and design. She studied how the Native Americans created their art. She learned how they constructed their buildings.

It was a time when few women explored the West. But Mary set out to find ancient Native American ruins. She even hired pilots to fly her over the territory. This air research method was ground-breaking! Wilbur and Orville Wright had only had their first successful flight the previous year.

After studying the authentic structures, Mary tried to recreate them exactly. Her Hopi House had tiny windows to let in a minimum of light. This characteristic was true of Hopi structures. She also had each of the rooms built with Hopi-style ceilings, made of saplings, grasses, and twigs. The walls were plastered with mud. Small fireplaces were built in the corners.

Her second Grand Canyon project was Hermit's Rest in 1914. The building was supposed to be a rest stop on Santa Fe railroad's tour of the canyon. Mary wanted her buildings to look as if they had always been part of the land. She even blackened the ceiling stones with soot. It looked as if travelers had built fires and rested there for years.

Mary had a good marketing sense. She knew that tourists always loved a good story. So she made up stories about her creations. One was about an old hermit who used to live by the Grand Canyon. He acted as a guide for tourists who wanted to explore the Canyon in the 1890s. Mary tied this old tale to Hermit's Rest to attract more tourists.

She also included a story when she designed the Phantom Ranch in 1922. It was built on the site of an old camp that President Theodore Roosevelt had built when he was exploring the Grand Canyon in 1903. It was once called the Roosevelt Camp. Mary changed the name to Phantom Ranch. She thought the name was more exciting. It suggested there were ghosts who roamed through the canyon.

Roosevelt's name would remain linked with the Grand Canyon. As president, he had 800,000 acres in and around the Grand Canyon set aside as a National Monument in 1908. A month after his death in 1919, Congress formally declared the Grand Canyon a national park.

Mary's attention to detail was evident in the Bright Angel Lodge built in 1935. Its most notable feature is its floor-to-ceiling "geological" fireplace. Mary had mules haul stones up from the canyon floor. Then, stone by stone, she layered the fireplace walls in the same order as the strata in the canyon walls.

In 1928, Fred Harvey asked Mary to design the "last great railway hotel." It was called La Posada in Winslow, Arizona. At this time, Winslow was the southwestern hub of the Santa Fe Railroad. The famous Route 66 also ran through Winslow. Mary built La Posada as a Spanish-style hacienda for a made-up family. The hotel had rooms for 70 guests. It had three restaurants and eight acres of gardens. It was built at the height of the Great Depression, but survived because it had many wealthy and famous guests.

Mary also created La Fonda Hotel in Santa Fe, New Mexico; the El Navajo Hotel and Railroad Station in Gallup, New Mexico; and the Painted Desert Inn in Painted Desert, Arizona. She designed beautiful interiors for Union railway stations in Chicago, Kansas City, St. Louis, and Los Angeles. She even designed the inside of the Cochiti dining car for the Super Chief train.

Mary is known for her sense of history and landscape. She used Hopi, Zuni, Navajo, and Mexican designs in all of her work. Many of her best designs were copied by other architects. Between 1920 and 1940, many of the structures in our national parks were built using native stone and wood. This style came to be known as National Park Service Rustic.

Mary Jane Colter retired in 1948. She lived in Santa Fe, New Mexico. She died ten years later at age 88. Her legacy allows us to both experience and preserve the architecture of the American West.

Her Grand Canyon structures include:

Hopi House, 1905

Hermit's Rest, 1914

Lookout Studio, 1914

Phantom Ranch, 1922

Watchtower at Desert View, 1932

Bright Angel Lodge, 1935

Remembering the Facts

1. In what states did Mary spend her childhood?

2. How did Mary convince her mother to let her attend art school?

3. How did Mary work to pay for her classes in art school?

4. How did Mary keep her promise to her mother after she finished art school?

5. Who was Fred Harvey?

6. How did Mary's career with Fred Harvey begin?

7. Where is Mary most well-known for her architecture?

8. How did Mary draw tourists to her creations?

Understanding the Story

9. Why do you think Mary wanted to work for Fred Harvey?

10. Why do you think Mary did so much research before she began a project?

Getting the Main Idea

Why do you think Mary is a good role model for young people today?

Applying What You've Learned

Mary took a great deal of care to incorporate the landscape and historical and cultural traditions in her designs. Why do you think this was important to do?

Ka'iulani

Hawaiian Princess

We do not think of the United States as having kings and queens or princes and princesses. But once, briefly, we did have a real princess. She was Ka'iulani of Hawaii.

Ka'iulani's birth on October 16, 1875 was a happy day for the kingdom. Her great-uncle, King Kalakaua, had no children. So he named his sister (and Ka'iulani's grandmother), Liliuokalani, heir to the Hawaiian throne. Next in line was her daughter, Princess Likelike. Ka'iulani was the only child of Princess Likelike (pronounced "Lee-keh-lee-keh") and Archibald Cleghorn. Cleghorn was a wealthy businessman from Scotland. He became the Royal Governor of the island of O'ahu. The people were overjoyed about the newest young member of their royal family.

The name *Ka'iulani* means "the royal sacred one." Ka'iulani's father was a friend and advisor to the king. He was also an expert in growing plants and flowers. So the grounds around the princess's estate, Ainahau, were some of the most beautiful on the island.

There were giant turtles and peacocks to entertain Ka'iulani. She loved to explore. She was an expert horsewoman, surfer, and swimmer. She even dared to go beyond reefs where some men wouldn't go. She was not a spoiled child. People loved her.

Ka'iulani was very happy until her mother died. She was 11 years old at the time. Her father and grandmother decided it was time to send her to school in England. "Only there," her father said, "can you receive an education fit for a queen."

Ka'iulani tried to be very brave. It would be hard for her to leave her father, her family, and friends. She would miss her beautiful house and gardens.

Another Scotsman, author Robert Louis Stevenson, was visiting Hawaii at the time. King Kalakaua introduced Stevenson to Princess Ka'iulani's father. He thought the two Scotsman would have much to share. But it was Princess Ka'iulani and Stevenson who became great friends. She loved his stories. He admired her love of life. Robert tried to ease some of her fears about England. He told her many good things about the country.

Her father sailed with Princess Ka'iulani to San Francisco. There they boarded a train to travel across the United States. The two parted as she boarded another ship to cross the Atlantic Ocean.

She was happy once she finally arrived in England. The ocean voyage had been long. She had been seasick most of the time. Ka'iulani found that she loved school. She made new friends there. And she looked forward to being presented at the English court to Queen Victoria.

But, over time, letters from home filled her heart with sadness. American businessmen were trying to take control of Hawaii. They called the native Hawaiians "savages." They thought the Hawaiians could learn something from them.

The Americans wanted to take control of Hawaii. King Kalakana died trying to stop them. His sister became Queen Liliuokalani. She named Princess Ka'iulani next in line for the throne.

But it wasn't long before the Americans forced Queen Liliuokalani to give up the throne. They set up their own government. The Princess's guardian in England received a telegram declaring: "1. Queen deposed; 2. Monarchy abrogated; 3. Break news to the Princess."

Princess Ka'iulani did not know how to help her people. Friends suggested she speak directly to U.S. President Grover Cleveland. She could try to convince him of the injustice. Then he could stop the takeover.

"What can I do to influence one of the greatest nations on Earth?" Ka'iulani asked. "I'm only a 17-year-old student." But she could not let her people down. She had to try to meet with President Cleveland.

A few weeks later, Ka'iulani set sail for the United States. She explained her mission to news reporters in England and America. The public was thrilled to read about this young princess's courage.

President Cleveland, too, was impressed by her bravery. He agreed to try to stop the takeover. He would try to give the royal family their throne again.

Sadly, he was powerless against the Americans who had taken over Hawaii. The only way Cleveland could have stopped them was to send in the Army. He refused to do that. All he could do was prevent the takeover for as long as he was president.

Ka'iulani went home to try to comfort her people. Things were very different from when she had left for school. Her beautiful gardens were overgrown with weeds. Her people were sad.

After President Cleveland left office in 1897, Congress voted to turn over Hawaii to the United States. Hawaii was no longer a free nation. Ka'iulani and her people wept as the Americans cheered. The young princess worked hard to keep peace among her people. Sometimes it worked. But even she could not return her people's good spirit.

Ka'iulaini's health was failing. She still did not give up. In January 1899, she rode horses with friends into the mountains. They got caught in a storm. Soon the princess came down with a fever. She never recovered.

Princess Ka'iulani died at the age of 23. Some said it was from the fever. Others said it was from sadness. The Hawaiian people were overwhelmed with sorrow. Thousands of people—even her enemies—attended her funeral. This princess never lived to become a queen. But her memory lives on in the hearts and minds of all Hawaiians.

Remembering the Facts

1. What does the name Ka'iulani mean?

2. How was the princess entertained as a child?

3. Where did Princess Ka'iulani go after her mother died?

4. How did Robert Louis Stevenson help Ka'iulani?

5. What news did Ka'iulani get from home that caused her great sadness?

6. How did the princess try to stop the Americans?

7. How had Hawaii changed when Ka'iulani returned home?

8. What caused Ka'iulani's death?

Understanding the Story

9.   Why do you think it was important for Princess Ka'iulani to return to Hawaii?

10.   Why do you think the Hawaiians were sad when their country was taken over by the United States?

Getting the Main Idea

Why do you think Princess Ka'iulani is a good role model for young people today?

Applying What You've Learned

Princess Ka'iulani was brave, and she cared about her people. Write a paragraph explaining why you think a leader should have these two important traits.

Eleanor Roosevelt

Humanitarian

One of Eleanor Roosevelt's first memories was when she and her parents were on a cruise to Europe. Their ship collided with another ship in the fog and sank. Luckily, all the passengers were rescued by the other ship.

Eleanor was haunted by a fear of drowning for the rest of her life. But that was perhaps the only fear she could not conquer. One of her favorite mottoes was, "You must do the thing you think you cannot do."

Eleanor was born on October 11, 1884. Her mother and father were wealthy New Yorkers. Her father was a handsome sportsman. Her mother was very beautiful, but not a very kind person. "My mother was troubled by my lack of beauty," Eleanor once wrote. "She tried to instill perfect manners in me to make up for my ugly-duckling appearance."

Just before Eleanor's eighth birthday, her mother died of diphtheria. She was only 29. Eleanor moved to her grandmother's house.

Eleanor and her father wrote lots of letters to each other. But then he died when she was ten.

Eleanor's grandmother's house was a gloomy place. She had raised four children of her own. By the time Eleanor came along, she was worn out. She always said "no" to anything Eleanor might ask.

Eleanor's life changed when she was 15. She went to Allenswood, a private school near London, England. The headmistress was a gifted teacher. Eleanor said, "She shocked me into thinking, and that was a very good thing." Eleanor learned to care about social injustice and how to voice her strong opinions. One of Eleanor's most famous quotes is: "No one can make you feel inferior without your consent."

Eleanor spent three very happy years at Allenswood. But at 18, she had to return to New York. She had to prepare for her debut. It was common for wealthy young girls to be presented to society at a gala ball in New York City.

Eleanor was soon bored with just a social life. She began to volunteer in schools. She also joined a reform group called the Consumers League. They examined working conditions for women in New York. Eleanor visited factories where girls worked 12 to 14 hours a day, 6 days a week, for only $6 a week. She also visited "sweatshops." She saw children, 4 and 5 years old, working until they collapsed.

In 1902, Eleanor met her distant cousin Franklin D. Roosevelt on a train. They fell in love and were married in 1905. Eleanor's Uncle Ted (Theodore Roosevelt) was the president. He gave the bride away.

Franklin entered politics in 1910 by running for New York State Senate. He won. Eleanor and Franklin now had two children. A third child, Franklin D. Roosevelt Jr., died in 1909. The family moved to the state capital, Albany. Their house became a meeting place for politicians. Franklin valued Eleanor's opinions on many different issues.

Shortly into his second term as senator, Franklin was appointed Assistant Secretary of the Navy. The family moved to Washington, DC. Eleanor gave birth to two more children there. She took an active part in raising her children. She remembered how lonely her childhood had been. She did not want her children to feel the same.

In 1920, Franklin left the Navy to run for Vice President of the United States. This was the first election in which women had the right to vote. Franklin asked Eleanor to join him on the campaign trail. He lost, but it was just the beginning of national politics for the couple.

In the summer of 1921, Franklin came down with polio. He recovered, but his legs were paralyzed forever. While he was recovering, Eleanor traveled around the country. She made visits and gave lectures. She worked to keep the Roosevelt name in the public eye.

Then, in 1928, Franklin was elected governor of New York. Since Franklin could not walk, Eleanor went to places he could not. She became skilled at judging people's well-being. She visited people at their schools and at their jobs.

In 1932, Franklin was elected President of the United States. Eleanor was more than just a president's wife and White House hostess. She often spoke on the radio. She also met with members of the press.

Eleanor even held special press conferences where she invited women reporters only. At this time in history, women reporters were often not included in the president's press conferences.

In 1935, she began her own newspaper column. She called it, "My Day." She continued to write it until shortly before she died.

Eleanor was the first president's wife to fly. She visited coal miners in Appalachia. She visited migrant workers in California. She visited slum dwellers in Puerto Rico. She visited poor sharecroppers in the South. She cared about people's problems.

She also cared about racial injustice. Eleanor said of America, "We have poverty that enslaves and racial prejudice that does the same." She was an early advocate of civil rights. Without Eleanor's support, the famous black singer, Marian Anderson, would not have been allowed to perform at the Lincoln Memorial in 1939.

Franklin was the first president ever elected to four terms. Eleanor was at his side for each one. During World War II, she traveled around the world to comfort American troops and work for peace. She did not slow down after Franklin died in 1945.

The new president, Harry S. Truman, asked Eleanor to join the U.S. delegation to the first General Assembly of the United Nations. She was a member for eight years. As the first Chair of the Human Rights Commission, she helped to create the Universal Declaration of Human Rights. The document outlines the rights which people around the globe should have. It was adopted by the United Nation's General Assembly in 1948. It still stands today. Eleanor considered it one of her greatest successes.

Eleanor continued to advise leaders—kings, queens, and presidents. John F. Kennedy would not run for president without her support.

She died of tuberculosis in 1962. She was buried beside her beloved Franklin at their home in Hyde Park, New York.

Eleanor Roosevelt is remembered as a great humanitarian—truly a "First Lady of the World."

Remembering the Facts

1. What type of people were Eleanor's parents?

2. What changed Eleanor's life when she was a teenager?

3. Why did Eleanor leave school when she was 18?

4. What did Eleanor do when she grew bored with her social life?

5. Who gave Eleanor away when she married Franklin Roosevelt?

6. Why did Eleanor take an active role in raising their children?

7. How did Eleanor help Franklin after he was paralyzed from polio?

8. What did Eleanor do during World War II?

Understanding the Story

9.   Do you think Eleanor had a happy childhood?

10.   Why do you think so many people asked Eleanor for her advice?

Getting the Main Idea

Why do you think Eleanor Roosevelt is a good role model for young people today?

Applying What You've Learned

Write a short paragraph about what you would do if you were married to the president of the United States.

Georgia O'Keeffe

Artist

Georgia O'Keeffe was one of America's greatest artists. She lived to be nearly 100 years old. She painted bold, beautiful flowers, bones, mountains, and clouds.

Georgia was born on a farm in Sun Prairie, Wisconsin. She was one of seven children. Georgia was first attracted to painting when she saw a painting her grandmother did. It was a watercolor of a red rose.

In 1902, when Georgia was 15, her family moved to Williamsburg, Virginia. The principal of Georgia's school was one of the first to see her talent. She did not make Georgia do class artwork. Instead, she told her to paint whatever she wanted. Later, she told Georgia's mother that Georgia should go on to art school.

Georgia's mother agreed. Georgia began studying at the Art Institute of Chicago. Then she studied at the Art Students League in New York City. She learned to appreciate paint and color from the famous artist, William Merritt Chase. Georgia won the Art League's prize for one of her still-life paintings. But she felt held back by the style taught at the school. She withdrew and stopped painting for four years.

Georgia took a summer course with Alon Bement at the University of Virginia. He taught her a whole new technique. She learned about oriental design. She studied the balance between light and dark. She also learned the importance of filling the canvas. She paid careful attention to the space between shapes. And she studied the post-Impressionist artists. From this, Georgia learned how colors and shapes can have lives of their own. They are not always tied to real objects.

In the fall of 1915, she began to create a series of abstract charcoal sketches. Soon she had finished a small collection of work. Georgia shut herself in a room and placed her drawings against the walls. If one looked too much like another artist's work, she threw it out. She wanted to express her own ideas.

She sent the sketches to an old school friend, Anita Pollitzer. Georgia thought only Anita would see the sketches. But she learned that Anita had shown them to the famous photographer, Alfred Steiglitz. He was known for finding and exhibiting the best new art. He was so excited about Georgia's work that he hung her sketches in his gallery. Georgia was furious and demanded he take them down. Alfred convinced her that they should stay up.

Critics praised Georgia's work. They said it was some of the most unique American art of the time.

Georgia married Alfred in 1924. They lived in New York City and on his farm in Lake George, New York. Georgia painted in both places. She began to paint giant, close-up images of flowers. Some filled the entire canvas.

Alfred took over 500 photographs of Georgia. He continued to promote her artwork. But the city became too crowded and too noisy for Georgia. She was also bored with Lake George. She said, "The people live such pretty little lives, and the scenery is such little, pretty scenery."

In 1929, she was invited to spend the summer in Taos, New Mexico. After that, she returned every summer until 1940. Then she bought her own ranch in Abiquiu, New Mexico. After Alfred died in 1946, Georgia rarely returned to New York. She loved the wild, open country in New Mexico. She continued to live there and paint until she died in 1986.

Georgia once said that courage is the first thing an artist needs to possess. Georgia always showed courage. She often broke the rules. She became a fine artist when women were expected only to teach art. She filled huge canvases with thick, colorful paints.

In 1946, the Museum of Modern Art in New York City displayed a collection of her art. It was the first showing the museum had ever given a woman artist.

In 1977, Georgia received the Medal of Freedom from President Gerald Ford. A year before she died, President Ronald Reagan presented her with the National Medal of Arts.

Georgia O'Keeffe and her paintings inspire artists to look for what is unique in ordinary, everyday things.

Remembering the Facts

1. What objects would you find in Georgia's paintings?

2. When was Georgia first attracted to painting?

3. Who was one of the first to notice Georgia's talent?

4. Why did Georgia leave the Art Students League in New York City?

5. Why did Georgia put all her sketches against the wall in a room?

6. What happened when Georgia sent her sketches to her friend Anita?

7. Why did Georgia want to leave the city?

8. Where did Georgia live for the rest of her life?

Understanding the Story

9. Many of the people who supported Georgia O'Keeffe's career in art were women. How did these women help change her life?

10. How do you think growing up on a farm in Wisconsin influenced Georgia's artwork?

Getting the Main Idea

Why do you think Georgia O'Keeffe is a good role model for young people today?

Applying What You've Learned

Georgia O'Keeffe was a very strong and independent woman. Do you think these are important qualities for a leader to have? Write a paragraph explaining your answer.

Dorothea Lange

Photographer

Dorothea Lange was born in Hoboken, New Jersey, in 1895. Her mother worked as a librarian in New York City, just across the river from Hoboken. Dorothea went to a school that was close to her mother's library. This was in a neighborhood called the Lower East Side. Every day after school, Dorothea would wait in the library until her mother finished work.

The Lower East Side was full of immigrants from all over the world. Dorothea could look into their tenement houses from the library windows. She saw people talking, cooking, washing, sewing, working, and eating. "I looked into lives so strange to me," she said.

Dorothea watched and learned. She used her eyes like a camera. She focused on details: people's faces, hands, the way they stood, the way they related to one another. She studied these details to better understand people and their lives. She did not own a camera. She took pictures in her mind. But she knew that someday she would take photographs.

Dorothea was shy and quiet. She felt out of place among the immigrant children in her school. She had polio as a child. This caused her to walk with a limp. This also made her feel like an outsider.

When Dorothea was 12, her father left home. He never visited or wrote Dorothea. He never sent money to help support her and her mother. So Dorothea and her mother moved in with her grandmother.

Dorothea's mother was always busy working. She did not have time to keep track of Dorothea. Dorothea enjoyed this freedom. She liked roaming the streets of New York. She loved to watch all the different people. She visited Central Park and the Museum of Natural History. She went to plays and art shows.

Dorothea's grandmother taught her how to look at objects. She told Dorothea, "Of all the beautiful things in the world, nothing is finer than an orange. Look at how perfect it is just as a thing in itself."

When Dorothea graduated from high school, she said that she wanted to take pictures. Her mother was worried. She had never heard of a woman photographer. Young women in the early 1900s were teachers, not photographers.

But Dorothea persuaded famous portrait photographer Arnold Genthe to hire her as an apprentice. He taught her how to use a camera. He taught her how to set up lights for the best picture. Perhaps his greatest lesson was that an artist must understand his or her subject.

Dorothea got her first assignment when no one else in the studio was there to take a photograph. The customer was pleased with her work. Arnold was pleased, too.

At that time, Dorothea was taking a class at Columbia University. It was taught by another famous photographer, Clarence H. White. He taught Dorothea the fine points of photographing people.

A year later, Dorothea and a friend left New York City for San Francisco. She began doing some portrait work for a store in the city. Her pictures were such a success that she soon opened her own studio. She had a reputation for being honest and sincere. Her portraits showed more than just subjects; they showed people's lives.

In 1920, she married a famous painter, Maynard Dixon. They had two sons, Daniel and John. Their marriage lasted 15 years. Later, Dorothea married economist Paul Taylor.

In the fall of 1929, the stock market crashed. The Great Depression had begun. Within a year, one out of every four people was jobless. People could no longer afford luxuries such as Dorothea's portraits or Maynard's paintings.

One day while looking out her studio window, Dorothea saw a drifter walk by. She was curious about where he was going. So she followed him down the street. He joined a line of people waiting for free food. Dorothea went back for her camera. She took one of her most famous photographs, "White Angel Bread Line."

Suddenly, Dorothea knew that real life was in the streets—not in her studio. She began with photographs of jobless people in San Francisco. She took pictures of longshoremen on the waterfront and homeless people all over the city. Her new photographs were called documentary photos.

Paul Taylor was a professor of economics at the University of California, Berkeley. He first saw Dorothea's work in 1935. He wanted to improve living conditions for the migrant workers, sharecroppers, and farmers in California. Taylor had written about their difficult lives, with no result.

Dorothea began to photograph the conditions. Her photos captured the evidence Taylor needed. Another of her most famous photographs, "Migrant Mother," was taken at this time. It was a picture of a poor, hungry migrant mother and her children. The government took notice. They began working to improve the lives of migrant workers.

Dorothea Lange's work was praised by Eleanor Roosevelt. She received more assignments from Washington. She and Paul Taylor were sent by the Farm Security Administration to photograph and report on farmers and migrant workers. They traveled to California, Oklahoma, and the rural South.

In 1940, Dorothea received one of the first photography Guggenheim Fellowships to "photograph the American Social Scene." After the bombing of Pearl Harbor, she photographed the forced evacuation of Japanese Americans. These photos were seized by the Army. But now they are part of the National Archives in Washington, DC.

Dorothea was very busy for the next 20 years. She founded *Aperture*, a photography magazine. She traveled to photograph people for *Life* magazine. She went to Vietnam, Ireland, Pakistan, and India.

In 1965, the Museum of Modern Art in New York City created a major exhibit of Dorothea's photographs. Dorothea was diagnosed with esophageal cancer. She died just before the exhibit opened.

Dorothea Lange spent her entire life photographing people. When she died, she left an amazing collection of photographs. She showed the world the power of photography. She showed how to use the lens to explore, reveal, and understand human life.

Dorothea said that she lived life as her grandmother did. She saw beauty in ordinary, everyday things. She saw beauty in a line of laundry flapping in the wind, a bread line, or a farmer's hands.

Remembering the Facts

1. Why did Dorothea spend so much time as a child in the Lower East Side?

2. Why did Dorothea feel out of place in school?

3. What led Dorothea and her mother to move into her grandmother's house?

4. Name three things Dorothea did in New York City to enjoy her freedom.

5. How did Dorothea get her start in photography?

6. Why did Dorothea begin taking fewer pictures in her studio?

7. How did Dorothea's photographs help migrant workers?

8. What did Dorothea do in the last 20 years of her life?

Understanding the Story

9. Why do you think Dorothea photographed people instead of places?

10. What was significant about Dorothea Lange's photography?

Getting the Main Idea

Why do you think Dorothea Lange is a good role model for young people today?

Applying What You've Learned

Write a brief paragraph describing a person. Then draw a picture of that same person. Which example do you believe best shows the person? Explain.

Rachel Carson

Conservationist

In 1963, Rachel Carson was a quiet author. She was a devoted conservationist. She was known for her books about marine biology. They described life under the sea and along the seashore. But her new book, *Silent Spring,* caused an uproar. It warned the public about the harm chemical pesticides cause the natural environment.

Silent Spring proved that pesticides were very dangerous to life on Earth. People in the giant $250 million pesticide industry were outraged. CBS television planned a special interview with Rachel Carson. But three of the five sponsors withdrew their support before the show went on the air.

Farmers had always used some form of pesticides. Before World War II, they did little damage. After the war, many more toxic pesticides were made. In 1960 alone, over 638 million pounds were used. All of these deadly chemicals were dumped into the environment.

Rachel Carson was born in Springdale, Pennsylvania, in 1907. Her family's farm was hundreds of miles from the ocean. But Rachel always felt her "destiny was somehow linked with the sea."

Rachel's mother was a teacher. She taught Rachel to be aware of the beauty and mystery in nature. Rachel said, "I can remember no time when I wasn't interested in the out-of-doors and the whole of the world of nature ... I was a solitary child and spent a great deal of time in woods and beside streams, learning the birds and the insects and the flowers."

Rachel loved books. She thought she would be a writer. In fact, she had her first story published in *St. Nicholas Magazine for Children* when she was ten.

After high school, Rachel went to Pennsylvania College for Women (later Chatham College). She studied English. She thought it was the best way to become a writer.

One day, Rachel signed up for a course in biology. She needed the credit to graduate from college. She was fascinated by what she learned. So she decided to major in biology instead of English.

"Biology," she said, "has given me something to write about. I will try in my writing to make animals in the woods and waters where they live as alive and as meaningful to others as they are to me."

Women did not often study science in the 1920s. But Rachel did. She graduated with honors in 1929. Then Rachel got a scholarship from Johns Hopkins University. She got her master's degree in zoology in 1932.

She thought the best part of her studies were the summers she spent at the Marine Biological Laboratory. It was a center for marine research in Woods Hole, Massachusetts. Rachel loved the ocean. She loved its creatures and plants. More than ever, she knew she wanted to be a marine zoologist.

In 1935, both her father and her older sister died suddenly. Rachel had to support her aging mother and her sister's two orphaned sons. She found a job writing scripts for a radio program for the U.S. Bureau of Fisheries. She wrote about marine life.

They were very pleased with her scripts. They asked her to write more. She wrote an article, "Undersea," in 1937. It was published in the famous literary magazine, *Atlantic Monthly.*

Rachel published her first book, *Under the Sea-Wind,* in 1941. It explored ecology. It showed the different ways animals depend on one another. Critics praised the book. It was always Rachel's favorite of all her work.

Much of World War II was fought on—and under—the sea. So a new interest in oceanic research began. The military need to know about tides, currents, and topography of the ocean bottom.

The U.S. Bureau of Fisheries was renamed the U.S. Fish and Wildlife Service. Rachel became editor-in-chief in the Office of Information. All new research in oceanography had to cross her desk.

Rachel was one of the first two women allowed to join the crew of *Albatross III.* This was the U.S. government's marine research vessel.

In 1951, Carson published her second book, *The Sea Around Us.* This time she wrote about the world's oceans. She covered the oceans from their origins billions of years ago, through the present time. The book was a huge success. It won many awards. It even won the National Book Award. The book became a best-seller in the United States. And it was translated into 32 different languages around the world! Then it was made into a documentary movie. The movie won an Academy Award.

The Edge of the Sea was published in 1955. It was also a best-seller. In it, Rachel wrote about the ecology of shore life along the Atlantic seaboard.

Silent Spring was very different from Rachel's earlier books. She knew that her argument against pesticides such as DDT would create lots of debate. But she could not keep silent. Rachel spoke before Congress in 1962. She urged them to create new laws to protect the environment.

President John F. Kennedy read her book. He ordered his Science Advisory Committee to create a special panel. This panel was to investigate the effects of pesticides on the environment.

Rachel Carson died of breast cancer two years after *Silent Spring* was published. She did not live to see the law that banned DDT. She was not aware of the many awards her book received. She did not hear the praises of those who read it. Supreme Court Justice William O. Douglas said, "*Silent Spring* is the most important chronicle of this century for the human race."

Sixteen years after she died, Rachel was awarded the Presidential Medal of Freedom. It is the highest award an American civilian can receive. *Time* magazine voted Rachel one of the "100 Most Influential People of the Century."

Rachel Carson is gone, but she still has an impact today. In 2006, former Vice President Al Gore presented a documentary titled *An Inconvenient Truth.* This movie showed Al Gore's effort to increase public awareness of global warming. Al was influenced by Rachel Carson. He says that reading *Silent Spring* made him much more aware of the environment.

Rachel Carson began the environmental movement. Without her efforts, the earth may have been a very different place today.

Remembering the Facts

1. Before Rachel went to college, what did she want to become?

2. What caused Rachel to change her major in college?

3. What was Rachel's favorite part of her studies?

4. What was the significance of Rachel joining the crew of *Albatross III*?

5. What book is Rachel most famous for?

6. What was this book about?

7. How did Rachel begin the environmental movement?

8. How has Rachel's book affected the environmental movement today?

Understanding the Story

9. Why did Rachel find marine zoology so rewarding?

10. Do you think Rachel was against people who make their living from pesticides? Or was she against what the pesticides do to the environment? Explain.

Getting the Main Idea

Why do you think Rachel Carson is a good role model for young people today?

Applying What You've Learned

It can be very hard to take a stand against something that makes money. If you knew that something that made people wealthy was also damaging our world, how would you argue on behalf of the world?

Ella Fitzgerald

Singer

Ella Fitzgerald was called America's "First Lady of Jazz." She won 13 Grammy awards and sold more than 40 million albums in her lifetime. But before she sang, she thought she wanted to be a dancer.

Ella was born in Newport News, Virginia, on April 25, 1917. Shortly after she was born, her father left home. Ella and her mother moved to Yonkers, New York.

Ella's childhood was not easy. Her mother worked in a Laundromat, and did some catering to support her family. But Ella's mother always had some time left in her day for music. She loved to listen to the radio. She collected records of the singers she liked best. Ella often sat beside her mother as she listened. Soon Ella began to sing along and dance.

In 1932, Ella's mother died from injuries from a car accident. Ella went to live with her aunt. Ella was not happy and she began to get in trouble with the police. She was sent to a reform school. But she ran away. At age 15, she was alone with no place to go. She knew she had to turn her life around.

She dreamed about dancing. One day she entered a talent contest. It was called the Amateur Hour at the famous Apollo Theater in Harlem, New York City. Ella planned to dance on stage. But once the curtain went up, she froze. Her feet felt like lead. Knowing the audience would not be patient, Ella finally burst into song. She did not feel so awkward singing. It was one of her mother's favorite songs, "Judy." The audience loved it. When Ella finished, they demanded an encore. She launched into another song.

This moment was a turning point in Ella's life. The audience loved her. She won first prize. She said, "I knew right then that I wanted to sing before people for the rest of my life."

Ella went on to win many more talent shows. Then one night in 1935, the famous drummer and band leader, Chick Webb, heard her. He hired her to sing with his band. Her pay was $12.50 a week!

Ella was, of course, a big hit. A pop music critic wrote, "The guys [in the band] loved her, she loved the guys, and the whole spirit of the band picked up.... She was dedicated to her music, never fully ready to recognize her own greatness but forever encouraging the talents of others."

In 1938, Ella and Chick Webb wrote a "swing" variation on the nursery rhyme, "A Tisket, a Tasket." Ella recorded it. It was her first huge success. It sold a million copies. It hit the top of the music charts. It stayed on top for 17 weeks! Ella was a national star when she was just 21 years old.

Chick Webb died in 1939. Ella took his place in the band. She became one of the first female bandleaders in history. Then many of the band members were drafted into the Army during World War II. So Ella did solo acts in nightclubs around the country. She also recorded more songs.

In 1946, Ella met bassist Ray Brown. They fell in love and were soon married. Later, they adopted a son.

Ella's mentor was Norman Grantz. She sang in his "Jazz at the Philharmonic" tours in the United States, South America, Asia, and Europe. The crowds were crazy about her music.

Ella had a long career ahead of her. Her vocal range spanned three octaves. She also perfected a unique singing style called *scat*. Scat is a wordless musical improvisation. As Ella sang, she used her voice to imitate the horns in the band. She loved to imitate the rhythm and sound of Dizzy Gillespie, a former trumpet player in her band. Gillespie was on his way to becoming one of the greatest trumpet artists in jazz history.

Ella recorded songs from many famous American composers. She performed with jazz greats Louis Armstrong, Duke Ellington, and Count Basie.

For years Ella toured around the world performing in jazz concerts. She often toured over 40 weeks out of the year.

In 1985, she collapsed from exhaustion. The following year, she had to have quintuple bypass surgery on her heart. She had to cut her number of performances to two or three a month.

She was also diagnosed with diabetes. Her doctors urged her to stop performing. Ella refused. Because of her diabetes, she later had to have both legs amputated. But Ella continued to perform. Ella died at her home in Beverly Hills, California, in 1996.

Ella Fitzgerald won many awards and honors. She won the National Medal of Arts and the Presidential Medal of Freedom. After her death, a postage stamp was issued with Ella's portrait on it.

In life, Ella was quite shy. People asked her how she had such a successful career with hardly any formal music training. She said, "I've always felt that where I got my education was with the musicians."

Ella Fitzgerald sang for more than 70 years. She never officially retired. She once said she might retire if people didn't want to hear her anymore. But that never happened.

Remembering the Facts

1. How was Ella first introduced to music?

2. What was Ella's life like after her mother's death?

3. How did Ella get her start singing?

4. Who gave Ella a job singing in a band?

5. What was significant about Ella becoming the band leader after Chick's death?

6. What unique singing style was Ella famous for?

7. Why did Ella have to cut back on her number of performances?

8. What happened when Ella was diagnosed with diabetes?

Understanding the Story

9. Ella Fitzgerald was just as popular with other performers as she was with her audience. Why do you think that was so?

10. Music was a very important part of Ella's and her mother's lives. Can you understand why?

Getting the Main Idea

Why do you think Ella Fitzgerald is a good role model for the youth of today?

Applying What You've Learned

Bursting into song was a very brave thing for Ella to do when she froze at the talent contest. Write a paragraph explaining what you would have done in this situation.

Rosalyn Sussman Yalow

Nobel Prize-Winning Doctor

The Nobel Prize is one of the world's greatest awards. It is named after Alfred Nobel of Sweden. He became a millionaire after he invented dynamite. Perhaps Nobel felt guilty about having invented such a deadly weapon. Before he died, he said, "I want all my money to be used to establish an annual award for the person who has done the most to benefit the world community."

The first awards were given in 1901. Since then, 768 have been awarded to scientists. Only 33 of those scientists are women. Rosalyn Sussman Yalow was one of those women. In 1977, she became only the second woman to win the prize in medicine.

Dr. Yalow was honored for her development of RIA, or radioimmunoassay. This is a test that measures hormones, viruses, enzymes, drugs, and hundreds of other biological substances. It helps detect disease.

Rosalyn Sussman was born in New York City on July 19, 1921. Her father, Simon Sussman, was a first-generation American. His family had moved to America from the Ukraine. Her mother, Clara Zipper, was four when her family moved to America from Germany.

Simon started his own paper and twine business. He lived in the Lower East Side of New York City. This was largely an immigrant community. Simon married Clara. They had two children, Alex and Rosalyn.

The Sussmans were poor. But they made the most of what they had. There was some money for Saturday movies and baseball games. And, once a week, Rosalyn and Alex would go to the public library and load up on books. Simon and Clara were not able to attend high school, but they wanted their children to go to college.

Rosalyn was a bright child. She taught herself to read before kindergarten. She loved math and was very good at it. She skipped several grades in school.

When Rosalyn was eight, she started helping her mother with her home sewing business after school. They made collars for women's dresses. Rosalyn's job was to turn the pieces of cloth while her mother ironed them.

Rosalyn went to all-girls' schools. She loved math and science and, above all, chemistry. She liked to sort out problems and puzzles.

At 15, she entered Hunter College in New York City. There, she took her first physics course. She also learned about Madame Curie. Curie was the only woman to receive two Nobel Prizes (one for Physics and one for Chemistry). Rosalyn knew she wanted to devote her life to physics.

Rosalyn was also influenced by Enrico Fermi. He was a guest lecturer at Hunter at the time. Fermi was the first physicist to split the atom. Later, his work in nuclear fission led to creating the first atomic bomb.

Rosalyn graduated with high honors as Hunter College's first physics major. She wanted to go on to graduate school. But all of her applications were turned down because she was a woman and a Jew. They said she'd never be able to get a job with two such "handicaps."

Finally, Rosalyn took a secretarial job at Columbia University. This job would allow her to take graduate courses there, for free. But she only stayed a few months. She was offered a job as a teaching assistant at the University of Illinois. It was 1941. There was an opening because so many men were fighting in World War II.

She was the only woman out of 400 men in the College of Engineering. She was also one of only three Jews. Another was Aaron Yalow. They met on the first day of graduate school. Two years later, they were married.

Rosalyn and Aaron had two children, Benjamin and Elanna. Rosalyn worked while raising them. She worked hard to balance her personal and professional lives.

The Yalows received doctoral degrees in physics from the University of Illinois in 1945. Then they moved back to New York. Rosalyn returned to Hunter College as a physics professor until 1950.

Rosalyn later worked as a researcher at the Bronx Veterans Administration Hospital. There she developed the hospital's radioisotope service. She also began research work with Dr. Solomon A. Berson.

In 1959, Dr. Yalow and Dr. Berson discovered RIA by chance. They had been trying to measure the amount of insulin in adult diabetics. They soon realized that RIA could detect and measure insulin. By using radioscope tracers, the RIA could measure better than any other process. It measured to the billionth of a gram!

A member of the Nobel committee said the accuracy of RIA was like being able to detect "half a lump of sugar in a lake about 62 miles long and wide and 10 miles deep." Today, RIA is used to test for hundreds of different medical problems. It is used in laboratories all over the world.

Dr. Yalow and Dr. Berson could have patented the process. They would have made millions of dollars. But they decided not to. It was far more important for others to be able to use this valuable tool than for them to make money from it.

Dr. Yalow and Dr. Berson were research partners for 22 years. Dr. Berson died in 1972. Had he lived, he could have shared the Nobel Prize with Dr. Yalow.

Rosalyn was elected to the National Academy of Sciences in 1975. In 1976, she was the first woman ever to win the Albert Lasker Prize for Basic Medical Research.

In 1997, Rosalyn was inducted into the Women in Technology International Hall of Fame. Today, she continues to teach at the Mount Sinai School of Medicine in New York.

Speaking for all women at the Nobel ceremony, Dr. Yalow said, "We must believe in ourselves or no one will. We must match our aspirations with competence, determination, and courage to succeed, and we must feel a personal responsibility to ease the path of those who come after us."

Remembering the Facts

1. What is the Nobel Prize?

2. Why was Dr. Rosalyn Yalow awarded the Nobel Prize?

3. Rosalyn's mother and father were first-generation Americans. What countries did their families come from?

4. Name two ways Rosalyn showed she was a bright child.

5. Why were Rosalyn's applications to graduate school turned down?

6. Why did Rosalyn take a secretarial job at Columbia University?

7. How did Dr. Yalow and Dr. Berson discover RIA?

8. What could Dr. Yalow and Dr. Berson have done to make more money on their discovery?

16 Extraordinary American Women

Understanding the Story

9. Dr. Yalow had to deal with a great deal of prejudice during the course of her career. How do you think she was able to overcome this and go on to help others?

10. RIA was discovered by accident while Dr. Yalow and Dr. Berson were investigating another medical problem. How do you think scientists keep their minds open for such new discoveries while they are working on other problems?

Getting the Main Idea

Why do you think Dr. Rosalyn Yalow is a good role model for the youth of today?

Applying What You've Learned

It was generous of Dr. Yalow to speak out for all women at the Nobel Prize ceremony. Do you think it is important for leaders to share the spotlight like this? Write a paragraph or two about what you would do if you received a Nobel Prize.

Nikki Giovanni

Poet and Civil Rights Activist

Nikki Giovanni's first book, *Black Feeling, Black Talk,* was published in 1968. It was just one year after she graduated from college. Since then, her books, poems, essays, and recordings have moved people. Nikki has said, "I'm just a poet looking at the world and my response is to raise questions, challenge assumptions, and share what you've learned along the way."

Nikki was born in Knoxville, Tennessee, in 1943. Her given name was Yolande Cornelia Giovanni, Jr. Not long after she was born, Nikki's parents moved the family to Cincinnati, Ohio. They lived in Lincoln Heights. It was an African-American neighborhood.

The Giovannis were poor, but Nikki didn't think so. They did not have indoor plumbing. But they had hundreds of books and a piano in their small house.

Nikki's father struggled help his family. But the house was full of emotion. Nikki hated to see her parents arguing so much. The summer before she was to enter high school, she called her grandmother, Louvenia, in Knoxville. She asked if she could come for a visit. Once Nikki was there, she asked her grandparents if she could stay. And she did—for three years! Then, as long as her grandmother was alive, she returned every summer.

Nikki helped with household chores. She also helped with Louvenia's social, political, and charitable activities. African Americans were often needed in town to protest racial unfairness. Louvenia sent Nikki to help.

Maybe a sick friend needed food or care. Louvenia sent Nikki to help. Nikki began to have strong ties to her family and her black community. Nikki calls the lesson "a strong sense of giving something back."

Another person who had a big influence on Nikki's life was Miss Alfreda Delaney, her high-school English teacher. Miss Delaney had Nikki read books by African-American authors. She told her to write about what she had read. Nikki learned that a writer could make a difference.

Nikki was a very bright student. She entered Fisk University when she was just 17. But there, her feisty nature got in her way. She was in constant trouble with the dean of women. Once, Nikki left campus without asking for the dean's permission. Nikki was going to Thanksgiving dinner at her grandparents' house. The dean dismissed her from school.

It was three years before Nikki returned to Fisk. By then, Fisk had a new dean of women. This dean supported Nikki's writing and political activities. Nikki set up a chapter of the SNCC (Student Nonviolent Coordinating Committee) on campus. She got involved in the black arts movement. She also edited *Elan*, a student literary journal.

In 1967, Nikki graduated from Fisk. Her grandmother died two months later. So Nikki moved back to Cincinnati. She wrote to cope with her grief.

Within a year, she had finished a collection of poems. They became her first book, *Black Feeling, Black Talk*. She borrowed the money to publish it.

Nikki organized Cincinnati's first Black Arts Festival. It was a festival that celebrated black art and artists.

By the end of 1968, Nikki had completed most of the poems for her second book. She titled the book *Black Judgment*. She published it with the money she had earned from the sales of her first book and a grant from the Harlem Arts Council.

Nikki was then awarded a grant from the National Endowment for the Arts. She moved to New York City to enroll in the School of Fine Arts at Columbia University. But her professors at Columbia told her she couldn't write! She left the program.

In 1969, Nikki gave birth to her son, Thomas Watson Giovanni. She began teaching at Rutgers University across the river in New Jersey.

Next, Nikki edited a collection of poetry titled *Night Comes Softly.* It was one of the first anthologies of poetry by an African-American woman. During this time, she was becoming more and more famous. *Ebony* magazine named Nikki "Woman of the Year."

In the first ten years of her writing career, Nikki published twelve books. She also recorded five albums. One of them, *Truth Is on Its Way,* was a best-seller. It sold more than 100,000 copies in six months. The album combined Nikki's poetry with traditional gospel spirituals. The album was awarded Best Spoken Word Album of the Year from NARTA (National Association of Radio and Television Announcers).

Nikki became very popular. She knows that most people do not read poetry books. So Nikki takes her words "on the road." Nikki speaks in cities, towns, churches, YMCAs, classrooms, and bookstores around the world.

Since 1987, Nikki has been on the faculty of Virginia Tech University. There she is a "University Distinguished Professor."

Nikki Giovanni speaks with fluency and joy on behalf of all people. She believes that poetry can bring about change. She says, "Always poems are written because ... the heart explodes with the necessity to bare itself in the hope that others might see.... Poetry can define the life or lack of life that we are leading."

In 2007, the president of Virginia Tech asked Nikki to do an important job. He asked her to speak at the convocation ceremony. The ceremony was dedicated to the 33 students who were killed on the campus earlier in the year.

Thousands attended the ceremony that day. Even President Bush and First Lady Laura Bush were there. Nikki recited a poem she had written for the event. Despite all the sorrow, the poem celebrated the world of Virginia Tech. As she finished the poem, everyone stood up. They began to chant the football team's cheer, "Go Hokies!" Nikki's words had restored hope to the grieving students and families.

Nikki's work is a celebration of African-American life. Today, she has written over 30 books, and dozens of poems and articles. One of her favorites is a picture-book edition of her poem, "Knoxville, Tennessee." It is a book that describes, in words and pictures, a happy homecoming in Knoxville.

Remembering the Facts

1. Why did Nikki go to live with her grandmother?

2. How did Miss Alfreda Delaney influence Nikki?

3. Why did Nikki have trouble at Fisk University?

4. What happened shortly after Nikki graduated from Fisk?

5. How did Nikki publish her first book?

6. Why did Nikki leave Columbia University?

7. Name three places that Nikki speaks around the world.

8. What was Nikki asked to do in 2007?

Understanding the Story

9. Why did Nikki not think her family was poor?

10. Who were the most important people in Nikki's life?

Getting the Main Idea

Why do you think Nikki Giovanni is a good role model for young people today?

Applying What You've Learned

Write a short paragraph describing how you think Nikki has lived up to her grandmother's lessons about the importance of giving something back to your family and your community.

Donna Karan

Fashion Designer

The newspapers have called Donna Karan the "Queen of Seventh Avenue." Seventh Avenue is the heart of the fashion design district in New York City. In fact, it is the heart of American fashion. Donna's success in the competitive world of fashion design is based on her philosophy: "I want to give the woman her own personal style so that her personality supersedes the clothes, and that she and her own feelings come through…"

Many ask Donna how she came to be so successful. Donna says, "Fashion is something that's in your blood." It's always been part of her life.

Donna was born in Queens, New York, in 1948. Her mother, Helen, was a fashion model. Her father, Gabby, was a well-known tailor in New York City. He often made clothes for celebrities. Sadly, Donna's father was killed in a car accident when she was three years old. "Sometimes," Donna says, "I feel my mother left me then, too." Her mother had to work hard to support Donna and her older sister.

Donna was not very popular in school. Kids called her "Popeye" and "Spaghetti Legs." She did not like many of her classes. But she did like art class. While in school, she created her first fashion collection by tracing patterns around her own body.

One summer she pretended to be older than 14 to get a job at a local clothing store. She loved her work. It gave her "a sense of what people looked good in and what they didn't."

In 1968, Donna was accepted at the Parsons School of Design in New York City. One of her classmates was Louis Dell'Olio. They became great friends. Later, they would be long-term business partners.

In her second year at Parsons, she got a summer internship at Anne Klein's fashion design house. In the 1960s and 1970s, Anne Klein made popular clothes for women. They were clothes that women could feel comfortable working and moving in. Anne liked Donna's work so much that she hired her full-time. Soon she made Donna her associate designer. Donna went back to Parsons for her bachelor of arts degree in 1987.

During this time at Anne Klein, Donna met Mark Karan. He owned a clothing boutique in Miami Beach, Florida. The two fell in love and were married. The marriage lasted for ten years.

Donna and Mark had a daughter. They named her Gabby, after Donna's father. Gabby was born just days before Anne Klein died of cancer. Donna now had a new baby to take care of and a business to run.

With a new baby, it was hard to get into work every day. So Donna's employees brought work to her. They sent the clothes right to her home.

Finally, Donna returned to the office. Anne Klein had a new owner. He was Tomio Taki, a Japanese man in the textile business. He made Donna chief designer. At age 26, Donna was already head of a major New York fashion house.

Less than six weeks after Anne Klein died, Donna presented her first collection as chief designer. It seemed like a miracle. And it was an instant hit. The audience gave her a standing ovation. They cheered for her designs, but also for her efforts to get the collection out on time. The Council of Fashion named her "Designer of the Year."

The following year, Donna made Dell'Olio her design partner. In 10 years, they built the company from a $10 million business into a $75 million business. It was a great success!

In 1985, Donna created her own company called Donna Karan New York. Her first collection won high praise from fashion critics. She continues to get good reviews with each collection she designs. One critic has said, "She's the only female world-class designer in the United States."

Donna never sells clothing that she would not wear herself. She said, "I'm a working woman. I need to make my life easier. I don't have time to spend hours selecting outfits to wear each day." She wants her clothes to reflect real life.

Donna identified the key pieces of any woman's wardrobe. From these "seven easy, essential pieces," she created a system in which each piece (skirt, pants, blouse, and jacket) fit with the others. The clothes did not go out of style quickly. A woman could wear her favorites until they fell apart. No one had to buy a whole new wardrobe every season.

In 1988, Donna launched a new line of clothes called DKNY. This is a less expensive collection. It is for women who want to look stylish, but don't want to pay the high price of designer clothing.

Three years later she launched a collection for men. Her second husband, sculptor Stephen Weiss, became her business partner. As vice president of the company, he put his artwork on hold and helped her create the collection for men. A lot of people thought men would not buy clothes with a woman designer's name on them, but they were wrong. Former president Bill Clinton is one of her best customers!

Donna's success was certain. So Stephen resigned in 1995 to return to his sculpting. One of his most famous pieces is a 3-ton apple installed beside the Westside Highway in New York City. Unfortunately, Stephen died of lung cancer in 2001. Donna has never remarried.

Donna's collections are now sold in over 300 of the best clothing stores in the United States. This includes stores such as Bloomingdale's and Macy's.

Donna built her company into $643 million business. She has won many awards. But this doesn't slow her down. She continues to work hard each year. "I have to reinvent myself every season," she says.

Donna Karan's fashions are not just about clothes. They are about people. Donna strives to make people feel good about themselves.

Remembering the Facts

1. How were Donna's parents involved in the fashion business?

2. Why did Donna not like school?

3. How did Donna get her very first start in fashion?

4. Who did Donna work for while in college?

5. How was Mark Karan involved in fashion?

6. When Donna's daughter was born, Donna was very overwhelmed. Why?

7. How did Donna find a way for women to avoid buying a new wardrobe every season?

8. How does Donna stay successful every season?

Understanding the Story

9. Why do you think family is so important to Donna?

10. Why was Donna so eager to make stylish clothes comfortable for women?

Getting the Main Idea

Why do you think Donna Karan is a good role model for young people today?

Applying What You've Learned

If you were designing clothes for today's busy women, what kind of wardrobe would you create?

Bonnie Blair

Speed Skater

Speed skater Bonnie Blair has won six Olympic medals. Five of those medals are gold! She has won more Olympic medals than any other American woman in any sport. She won her first gold medal in the 1988 Winter Olympics in Calgary, Canada. She won two more at the 1992 Winter Games in Albertville, France. And she won another two at the 1994 Winter Olympics in Lillehammer, Norway.

Bonnie Kathleen Blair was born on March 18, 1964, in Cornwall, New York. Skating was in her blood. Her five older brothers and sisters were all already skating when she was born. On the day of her birth, a skating meet was scheduled at the local rink. Some of the Blair children were in the race. Mr. Blair dropped Bonnie's mother off at the hospital and went on to the skating rink. He did not want to miss the meet. During the meet, the announcer's voice came over the loudspeaker: "Looks like the Blairs have another skater!" That was Bonnie's first "appearance" at a skating rink.

All the Blair children liked speed skating. The fancy moves in figure skating did not interest them. Bonnie's mother later said, "All Bonnie ever wanted out of skating was to skate and create the wind around her."

Bonnie's family moved to Champaign, Illinois, when she was two years old. By the time she was three, she was taking her first skating steps. Her brothers and sisters were great skaters. Almost as soon as Bonnie could stand up and walk, they took her to the ice rink. Her feet were so tiny they had to put a pair of skates on over her shoes. Bonnie remembers those first steps on the ice.

Bonnie entered her first official speed skating race at age four. When she was six, she was beating girls who were much older. At seven, she skated in the Illinois State Championships.

When Bonnie was 15, she made it to the United States Olympic trials. She just barely missed making the team for the 1980 Olympics in Lake Placid, New York.

Her coach advised her to go to Europe to train for the 1984 Olympics. Bonnie's family could not afford to send her there. So the town pitched in to help. Soon Bonnie was on her way to Europe. While training there, Bonnie continued her high-school studies. She was able to graduate from all the way across the Atlantic Ocean.

She made the 1984 Olympic Team and competed in Sarajevo, Yugoslavia. But it would be four more years before she won her first Olympic medal.

With the 1988 Winter Games in Calgary came gold. The event was the 500-meter race. Bonnie beat her opponent by just two-hundredths of a second. That was less than a foot! Her official time was 39.1 seconds. It was a world record for women.

She also won a bronze medal that year in the 1,000-meter event. Bonnie was the only U.S. athlete to win two medals. Her teammates asked her to carry the American flag in the closing ceremonies.

Bonnie won her third and fourth gold medals in the 500- and 1,000-meter races at the 1992 Olympics. She was the first woman to win gold medals in the same event in two consecutive Olympics.

Bonnie won two more gold medals at her fourth and last Olympics in Lillehammer, Norway. She competed in the 500- and 1,000-meter races again. She beat her own record of 39.1 seconds set at the 1988 Olympics.

She finished in 38.99 seconds. She had won more gold medals than any other American woman in Olympic history.

Bonnie is also the only Olympian, male or female, to win gold medals in the same event (500 meters) in three consecutive Olympics. Experts agree she is one of the greatest technical speed skaters in the world.

But it's not winning that Bonnie loves. It's the race itself. She entered an extra race—the 1,500-meter—in her free time at Lillehammer, just "for the thrill of competition."

Whenever possible, Bonnie's family and friends went to her competitions. More than 60 of them cheered her on in Norway. Her brothers and sisters have no regrets with their own skating. They are very proud of their little sister.

Sports Illustrated named Bonnie Blair "Sportswoman of the Year" in 1994. That was an important honor to Bonnie because she had grown up reading the magazine. The current issue was always in her house.

Bonnie retired from speed skating in 1995 on her 31st birthday. But she's kept busy since then. She married fellow speed skater Dave Cruikshank. She has been by his side through all his competitions. The couple has two children.

Retiring hasn't stopped Bonnie from being part of speed skating. She has been on the Board of Directors for U.S. Speed Skating. She has served on Olympic committees. She also wrote a book about her skating career.

Bonnie now spends much of her time as a motivational speaker. She tells her audiences to strive for their personal bests. She also donates her time to her charity, the Bonnie Blair Charitable Fund.

In 2004, Bonnie Blair was inducted into the United States Olympic Hall of Fame.

Remembering the Facts

1. What happened on the day of Bonnie's birth?

2. How old was Bonnie when she began skating?

3. How did Bonnie get to train in Europe?

4. How did Bonnie graduate from high school?

5. What was significant about the 1988 Olympic Winter Games in Calgary?

6. How many gold medals has Bonnie won?

7. After she retired, how was speed skating still a part of Bonnie's life?

8. How does Bonnie keep busy today?

16 **Extraordinary** American Women

Understanding the Story

9. Bonnie loves to skate, and not just for the medals. What do you think she likes best about this sport?

10. Do you think Bonnie was distracted or encouraged by the number of family and friends who showed up at her competitions?

Getting the Main Idea

Why do you think Bonnie Blair is a good role model for young people today?

Applying What You've Learned

Participating in Olympic events carries a lot of pressure as well as excitement. How would you feel if you were chosen to represent your country in an Olympic event?

Eileen Collins

Astronaut

Eileen Collins dreamed of flying as a little girl growing up in Elmira, New York. Elmira is called the "soaring capital of America." It is home to the National Soaring Museum. Eileen remembers her parents taking her and her siblings to watch the gliders. She was fascinated. She constantly thought about how much she would love to fly. Eileen was determined to make it happen one day.

Eileen was born on November 19, 1952. She had two brothers and a sister. Her parents were very supportive of her dream, but they didn't have enough money to pay for flying lessons. So Eileen lived her dream of flying through books. She read everything she could find about flying. She studied the pilots and their airplanes, beginning with the Wright Brothers. She learned the basics of flying. These would help her later, when she began to fly herself.

After Eileen graduated from high school, she enrolled in the local Corning Community College. She received an associate's degree in science in two years. She had worked hard there, and was rewarded with a scholarship to Syracuse University. She earned a bachelor of arts degree in math and economics in 1978.

At Syracuse, Eileen worked in a pizza parlor. She saved the money she earned. When she had saved $1,000, she went to the local airport. She asked the pilots to teach her how to fly.

Eileen graduated the same year that NASA first allowed women to join the astronaut program. Eileen's dreams became even bigger. She set her mind on becoming an astronaut.

Eileen had been a member of the AFROTC (Air Force Reserve Officers Training Corps) in college. As soon as she graduated, she was accepted into the pilot training program at Vance Air Force Base in Oklahoma. She completed her training.

Then Eileen became a flight instructor. She moved on to Travis Air Force Base in California. There, she continued to train other pilots. She also met her future husband, Pat Youngs. He was also an Air Force pilot. They later married in the Air Force Academy chapel.

In 1986, Eileen was invited to teach math at the U.S. Air Force Academy in Colorado Springs, Colorado. Eileen's experience and expertise was a rare find. She was a woman with both flying skills and academic credentials. She was a special role model for her students.

Eileen went on to become a test pilot at Edwards Air Force Base in California. During her tour of duty, she decided to go back to school. She received a master's degree in science from Stanford University.

In 1989, while still in school, she applied for the astronaut program. She was accepted. Eileen's career as an astronaut began with a number of support roles. She worked in flight engineering, landing and recovery, and as a Mission Control spacecraft communicator. But, she was still the only member of her class who was both a woman and a test pilot. NASA had more important roles waiting for her.

Her big moment came in 1995 when she flew as a pilot on the *Discovery* space shuttle mission. This was the first space shuttle to convene with the Russian space station, Mir. It was part of the new joint Russian-American space program.

Reporters asked her how the launch felt. She said she did not like sitting with her back to the rockets. The roar of their firing was very loud. She explained that it was much louder than it sounds on television or watching the launch in person. She felt as if she was surrounded by flames.

Once the shuttle broke through the earth's atmosphere, Eileen took a pencil out of her pocket. She wanted to see if it really did float. It did. She said, "To see that happen in real time—not in a simulator—was amazing."

Eileen made history in 1999. President Bill Clinton held a press conference at the White House. He announced that she would be the first woman to command a shuttle flight.

A reporter asked Eileen how much control a commander actually has. So much of the shuttle computer is controlled from the ground. Eileen said that the commander and crew always have to be ready to take over and fly the shuttle, in case any of the computer systems fail. They are all trained in flight simulators. These reproduce all kinds of problems that the crew has to be able to fix in seconds.

Eileen's 1999 mission was the shuttle *Columbia*'s last flight before its devastating accident in 2003. In that year, it disintegrated while re-entering Earth's atmosphere. Seven astronauts were killed.

Eileen's mission was a success. It was also an historic event for women in science. She was inducted into the National Women's Hall of Fame. The Hall of Fame is in Seneca Falls, New York, not too far from Elmira. While it was quite close to her hometown, Eileen had to travel thousands of miles through space to reach Seneca Falls!

One of Eileen's greatest challenges was commanding the 2005 *Discovery* shuttle. It was the first space mission since the *Columbia* disaster. The world was on edge. Though the future of the space program was at stake, Eileen did not hesitate.

During this successful mission, Eileen became the first astronaut to fly a shuttle through a 360-degree, nose-to-tail, pitch turn. This was a tricky and critical maneuver. Eileen's test pilot background made her crew feel secure. The astronauts aboard the space station had to photograph the underside of the shuttle. They needed a complete picture of the shuttle. This was to make sure that that there had been no damage to any part of it during take-off. They did not want the *Discovery* to suffer the same fate as the *Columbia*.

Eileen, now a colonel in the Air Force, retired in 2006. She has flown four successful space missions. She felt it was time to give others a chance to do the same.

Remembering the Facts

1. What is special about Eileen's hometown?

2. How did Eileen learn about flying when she was young?

3. How did Eileen earn money to take flying lessons?

4. What was significant about the year Eileen graduated from Syracuse?

5. How did Eileen meet her husband?

6. Why was the U.S. Air Force Academy in Colorado Springs so lucky to have Eileen as a math teacher?

7. What was the first thing Eileen did on her first mission when the shuttle got into space?

8. Why did Eileen retire from NASA in 2006?

Understanding the Story

10. How do you think Eileen felt about her space missions after the *Columbia* disaster?

11. Eileen was the first female in many roles: test pilot, shuttle pilot, shuttle commander. Do you think Eileen thought she should be awarded these firsts just because she was a woman?

Getting the Main Idea

Do you think Eileen Collins is a good role model for young people today?

Applying What You've Learned

Eileen was very brave to command the first space mission after the *Columbia* disaster. How would you have prepared to do this?

Ruth Bader Ginsburg

Supreme Court Justice

In 1973, Ruth Bader Ginsburg's daughter, Jane, wrote the following ambition in her high-school yearbook: "To see my mother sit on the U.S. Supreme Court."

Ruth Bader Ginsburg was born on March 15, 1933, in Brooklyn, New York. Her father, a fur dealer, owned a small store. Her mother was a homemaker.

Ruth grew up in a close and loving family. She had one older sister. But her sister died from meningitis at the age of six. Her parents had not been able to go to college. But they saw the importance of education. Ruth's mother often took her to the library. She saved up money for Ruth to go to college. Ruth's parents encouraged her to work hard for whatever she believed in. They felt that Ruth—or any young girl—should have the same opportunities in life that boys did.

Ruth was number one in her elementary school class. At age twelve, she wrote her first legal article, "Landmarks of Constitutional Freedom." It was printed in the school newspaper.

But Ruth had other interests, too. She was a baton twirler. She played the cello in the school orchestra. She was also the editor of the school newspaper.

Ruth did not have to use her mother's savings for college. Cornell University gave her a full scholarship because of her success in high school. Ruth's mother died of cancer the day before Ruth graduated from high school. But she died knowing that her daughter was going on to college.

Ruth met her future husband, Martin, during her first year at Cornell. They were married after graduation in June 1954. They both wanted to become lawyers.

Martin was a year older than Ruth. So he went to Harvard Law School first. His studies were put on hold when he was drafted into the Army in 1954. He and Ruth moved to Fort Sill, Oklahoma. Ruth got a job in the local Social Security office.

That job was her first experience with discrimination against women. As soon as her boss learned she was pregnant, he cut back her pay by three levels. Now more than ever, Ruth wanted to study law.

She decided to apply to Harvard. Martin would be returning there after he finished his two years of military service. Most people thought Ruth should be a teacher instead. Martin disagreed. But no woman had ever been admitted to Harvard Law School.

Ruth was determined, so she applied. She was accepted as one of nine women in a class of more than 500 at Harvard Law. Life was not easy for these first female law students. There was a great deal of prejudice against them. Even the dean of the law school said, "Do you realize that you are simply taking the place of a qualified man?"

Cancer struck Ruth's family again. During her second year at Harvard, Martin was diagnosed with testicular cancer. Ruth attended classes for him. She typed all his papers.

Through all of this, Ruth never missed a class of her own. And she still managed to take care of their young daughter, Jane.

Martin recovered and graduated from Harvard in 1958. He got a job with a law firm in New York City. Ruth wanted to keep her family together. So she transferred to Columbia Law School in New York.

There, she was one of ten women in the class. She was the first person—male or female—to work on both the *Harvard Law Review* and the *Columbia Law Review.*

She graduated—tied for number one in her class—in 1960. She wanted a job as a law clerk for a justice of the U.S. Supreme Court. The dean of Harvard Law recommended her for the position. He noted that Ruth was "one of his star students." Justice Felix Frankfurter turned her down instantly. He said, "I don't hire women."

This was the first of many rejections for Ruth. Even though she was at the top of her class, no one would hire her. She was a woman, she was Jewish, and she was a mother. These all worked against her. At that time, there was still prejudice against Jews. And employers thought it was impossible for mothers to have jobs and also care for their children.

Finally, Ruth got a job as a legal secretary. Then, in 1963, she was hired by Rutgers School of Law in New Jersey as a professor. She was one of the first 20 women ever hired to teach in an American law school.

When she became pregnant with her second child, Ruth wore baggy clothes so no one could tell. She did not want to be demoted again. Luckily, her son was born during the summer. She could return to teaching in time for fall classes.

At Rutgers, Ruth learned that female professors were paid less than men for the same work. She helped change this policy. Then she went on to argue several other cases on behalf of women. She changed the rule that forced women to quit their jobs when they became pregnant.

Ruth taught at Rutgers for nine years. Then she was hired by Columbia Law School as its first female law professor.

Ruth became a leading women's rights lawyer. She argued many sex discrimination cases for the ACLU (American Civil Liberties Union).

In 1980, President Jimmy Carter appointed Ruth to the U.S. Court of Appeals. It is the second highest court in the United States. There she was known for "being tough on crime, committed to free speech and freedom of religion, and supportive of civil rights." Then, in 1993, President Bill Clinton chose her for the Supreme Court.

In his historic announcement, President Clinton said, "Ruth Bader Ginsburg is the Thurgood Marshall of gender equity law…. Throughout her life she has repeatedly stood for the individual, the person less well-off, the outside in society, and has given these people greater hope by telling them they have a place in our legal system."

Jane's high-school yearbook wish had come true. Ruth became only the second woman to sit on the Supreme Court in its 212-year history. Sandra Day O'Connor was the first.

In 1999, Ruth had a cancer scare of her own. She was diagnosed with colon cancer. Fortunately, it was detected early. She fully recovered after her surgery.

In 2004, Ruth wrote the dissenting opinion for the Supreme Court's Bush vs. Gore decision.

Sandra Day O'Connor resigned in 2006. Ruth said she felt rather lonely being the only woman on the Supreme Court. But she does not wish to see another woman appointed to the court just because she is a woman. She says that she believes in equal rights for both women *and* men.

Remembering the Facts

1. How did Ruth's parents support and encourage her?

2. In addition to her studies, what were Ruth's other interests?

3. What made Ruth want to study law even more than she had before?

4. What did people tell Ruth she should do instead of going to law school?

5. What challenge did Ruth and Martin face while at Harvard Law?

6. What were the three reasons Ruth had a hard time finding a job?

7. How did Ruth handle her second pregnancy?

8. Who was the first female Justice of the Supreme Court?

Understanding the Story

9. Ruth Bader Ginsburg experienced much prejudice against women. How do you think that affected her legal decisions?

10. Where did Ruth get support for her career choices?

Getting the Main Idea

Why do you think Ruth Bader Ginsburg is a good role model for young people today?

Applying What You've Learned

Even though Ruth Bader Ginsburg experienced much prejudice, she never became bitter or lost her sense of fairness. If you had to work against the same biases, do you think you could remain so open-minded?

Susan Butcher

Iditarod Champion

A sense of adventure. Dogsledding expertise. The courage to journey through unchartered terrain. Grit and determination. All of these qualities made Susan Butcher a champion. She was only the second woman to win the famed Alaskan Iditarod dogsled race.

Susan was born and raised in Cambridge, Massachusetts. Home to the Harvard University, Cambridge was known for producing scholars—not mushers.

When she was a child, Susan got her first dog, a Siberian husky. Susan learned that her new puppy's mother was an Alaskan sled dog and the leader of a team. The dog's owner said, "Maybe you could teach this puppy how to pull a sled."

Susan became curious about sled dogs. She read a story about the Iditarod. She told herself, "I'm going to go up there and run that race."

Susan graduated from high school in 1972. She went to Colorado State University. There she studied veterinary medicine. She took all the classes she needed to be a veterinary technician. But Susan did not have the patience to carry on with her studies to become a doctor.

Susan left college in 1975 when she was 20 years old. She moved to Alaska. She wanted to follow her dream of dogsled racing and raising huskies. Susan instantly felt at home in Alaska.

She had a pilot with a small ski plane fly her in to a remote point. Her closest neighbor was 40 miles away! She settled in a cabin with no water and no electricity. Her first years were dedicated to learning how to survive in the wilderness. And she also raised and trained dogs. She had little money, so she had to build her own dogsleds.

In 1978, Susan ran her first race. She and her team finished in 19th place. She raced again in 1980 and moved up to the top five. In 1985, she was in the lead when she and her team collided with a moose. The moose killed two of her dogs and injured 13 others. But that didn't stop Susan.

The Iditarod is an annual dogsled race in Alaska. About 50 mushers and 1,000 dogs participate. Mushers and their dog teams cross about 1,150 miles in 8 to 20 days. The race takes place in March. It is grueling. They race in 100 mph winds and blinding snow. It is often as cold as 70 degrees below zero! The terrain is wild. The trail is not groomed. In fact, the lead team often has to blaze a new trail. They race from point to point through deep forests and mountain passes, across frozen tundra, rivers, and streams, and along the shore of the Bering Sea.

Though the conditions were brutal, Susan always saw the beauty in the race. She loved the sight of 16 huskies racing across the landscape under the glare of the sun or the glow of the northern lights.

Teams can run during the day or at night. There are 25 checkpoints along the trail where mushers must sign in. Rules require three absolute rest stops: one 24-hour layover, one 8-hour layover, and one 8-hour stop. Susan knew that the pace of the team was very important.

Alaskan huskies love to race. They are always eager to pass the teams ahead. But they, like the mushers, need to rest in order to complete the long race. Mushers have to be constantly aware of the dogs' needs. Susan was known for the care and training of her dogs. She would make sure they were all fed and lying down to sleep before she rested. Many said that she cared too much about her dogs to ever win the race.

Mushers need to be strong. The dogs are harnessed to the sled and each other. But there are no reins for the musher to control the dogs and steer the sled. A typical sled weighs from 150 to 200 pounds. Mushers must use verbal commands to direct the dogs: "gee" for right, "haw" for left, and "whoa" to stop.

In 1985, Susan married fellow dogsled racer, David Monson. When they weren't racing, they were raising huskies. They opened Trailbreaker Kennels in Eureka, Alaska. They later had two daughters, Tekla and Crisana.

Susan had her first Iditarod win in 1986. She also won the next two years. In 1989, she finished second. But Susan did not give up. She came back to win first place yet again in 1990. She had four first place finishes in five years! It was an astounding Iditarod record for any musher, male or female.

In 2005, Susan was diagnosed with acute myelogenous leukemia. She was taken to a hospital in Seattle, Washington, for chemotherapy. But she needed a bone marrow transplant.

The state of Alaska pulled together for their beloved champion. More than 1,100 Alaskans signed up to be donors. The Blood Bank of Alaska said there hadn't been this many donors since the terrorist attacks of September 11, 2001. Susan was honored. But she was also glad to know that so many of those donors would be able to help other sick people, too.

Susan remained hopeful that she would survive. She was surrounded with support from her loved ones. She worried about leaving her daughters without a mother at such a young age. But she knew they were strong and would be okay. She kept a journal for them to read if she died. She wanted them to remember her and know how she felt about them. She hoped that they would never have to read it.

Susan never quit fighting the cancer, but it was a fight she could not win. She died in August, 2006 at the age of 51.

In her memory, Susan's family created the Susan Butcher Family Center at the Providence Alaska Medical Center in Anchorage, Alaska. It is a special place where children can go while a parent is being treated for cancer.

Susan Butcher may be gone, but the mushing legend lives on in her family. Her daughter Tekla competes in some smaller dogsled races. Many say she has the spirit of her mother. And she's the spitting image of her, too!

Susan was at the 2007 Iditarod. Her husband spread her ashes over one of her favorite spots on the trail. Now she will be part of the Iditarod forever.

Remembering the Facts

1. When did Susan become interested in dogsled racing?

2. What did Susan first do when she moved to Alaska?

3. How did Susan lose her lead in the 1985 Iditarod?

4. Why was Susan criticized about the care of her dogs?

5. How many Iditarod races did Susan win?

6. What devastating news did Susan get in 2005?

7. Why was Susan happy to have so many people sign up to donate bone marrow?

8. What did Susan do for her daughters before she died?

Understanding the Story

9. What was Susan drawn to the Alaskan wilderness?

10. Why did so many Alaskans volunteer to donate their bone marrow to save Susan's life?

Getting the Main Idea

Why do you think Susan Butcher is a good role model for young people today?

Applying What You've Learned

Do you think you could survive in the Alaskan wilderness? How would you prepare yourself and a team of dogs to compete in the Iditarod?

Nancy Pelosi

First Woman Speaker of the House

Millions watched President George W. Bush deliver his State of the Union address in January 2007. He spoke to Congress and to the nation. It was an historic moment for Nancy Pelosi, for Congress, and for women everywhere. Never before had a woman sat beside the vice president as the president gave his speech.

Nancy Pelosi stepped up to the podium. There was loud applause from Democrats and Republicans alike. Nancy was the newly elected Speaker of the House of Representatives. On January 4, 2007, Nancy was elected to the position by the members of the house. She is the first woman in the history of the United States to reach such a powerful position. The president praised Nancy for her success.

Nancy Pelosi is just two steps away from the most powerful office in the world. If anything happened to the president and the vice president, she would become President of the United States.

Nancy Pelosi was born Nancy Patricia D'Alesandro in Baltimore, Maryland, in 1940. She grew up in the Little Italy neighborhood of the city. It is an area where people are very proud of their heritage. Fire hydrants are painted green, white, and red. These are the colors of the Italian flag.

Nancy was the youngest of six children. She was the only daughter born to Thomas D'Alesandro Jr. and his wife, Annunciata. Nancy was raised in a political family. They were proud to be Italian. But they were even more proud to be American. They believed in serving their country. And they took it very seriously.

Nancy's father was a member of the House of Representatives from 1939 to 1947. Then he was elected Mayor of Baltimore. Nancy was only seven. She held the bible at his swearing-in ceremony. He was Baltimore's first Italian-American mayor.

Nancy's father went on to serve three terms. He was a great man who was loved by the citizens. He was known for his sense of style. He was famous for his polka dot bow tie that he wore for good luck. Later, his son Thomas D'Alesandro III would also become Mayor of Baltimore.

The D'Alesandro's brick row house was an important place. People gathered to discuss the community, the city, and the state. Nancy learned politics from the ground up. She stuffed envelopes and did odd tasks to help with her father's campaigns. When she was 12, Nancy attended her first Democratic National Convention.

Nancy spent her childhood and teens listening to the people who came to see her father. Some were politicians. Others just wanted a job. They all needed her father's help. Nancy's mother pitched in, too. She learned early on how to balance her marriage, her children, the campaign, and serving the needs of her community.

Nancy attended Notre Dame High School for girls in Baltimore. She went to Trinity College, a Catholic college for women in Washington, DC. She earned her degree in 1962.

Nancy got a job as an intern for a Maryland senator. In 1963, she married Paul Pelosi. They had five children. In 1969, Nancy and Paul moved to San Francisco—Paul's hometown.

Nancy was a devoted wife and mother. At the same time, she did not neglect her political roots. She worked hard for the Democratic Party. She volunteered to help with political campaigns. She was a very good fund-raiser. By 1981, she had been named chair of the California Democratic Party.

Nancy had never run for political office herself. But in 1986, she took the step. She was 47, and her youngest child was in high school. Nancy ran for the House of Representatives from California's Eighth Congressional District. She was elected in 1987.

Sadly, her father died that same year. But Nancy would never forget what he taught her. He said that "public service was a noble calling."

Nancy used her new power to advocate for better pay for the working poor, for AIDS research, and for the Asian immigrant population in San Francisco. Her father had worked on behalf of the Italian immigrants in Baltimore; Nancy worked for the immigrants of San Francisco. She was an advocate for civil and human rights. In 1991, she protested the killings in China's Tiananmen Square. Today, she still believes we should limit our trade with China until it improves its human rights record.

Nancy is a skillful leader. She rose to powerful positions in the Democratic Party. In 2001, she was elected the minority whip in the House of Representatives. Nancy was the first woman to be elected to this position in the history of Congress. Then, in 2002, Nancy achieved another first. Minority leader, Richard Gephardt, decided to step down as minority leader. The House voted 177 to 29 for Nancy to take his place.

In 2006, the Democrats regained the majority in the House. Nancy achieved another first by being elected Speaker of the House.

As high as this position is, Nancy is still mindful of her roots. She paid a visit to her family home in Baltimore's Little Italy before her swearing-in ceremony. She was warmly welcomed by many who had known her as "Little Nancy, the Mayor's Daughter." She thanked old neighbors and new friends for their support and inspiration. The city renamed the street by her house Via Nancy D'Alesandro Pelosi.

But Nancy has a long track record of building support and partnerships among people with different opinions. She does not hesitate to use "her mother-of-five voice" when she needs to be heard.

Like her father, Nancy has been noted for her style, her ability to listen, and her eagerness to help others. Nancy's children and grandchildren were with her at her swearing-in ceremony. In her speech, Nancy promised to uphold the interests and well-being for "all of America's children."

Remembering the Facts

1. How many steps is Nancy away from becoming President of the United States?

2. Where did Nancy grow up?

3. How was politics part of Nancy's life growing up?

4. What did Nancy do after she graduated from Trinity?

5. Why did Nancy leave Maryland?

6. What was Nancy's first political office?

7. What did Nancy work for in public office?

8. When was Nancy elected as Speaker of the House?

Understanding the Story

9. How do you think Nancy's growing up in a political family influenced her career?

10. What skills does a mother of five bring to bear when Nancy tries to get political opponents to agree?

Getting the Main Idea

Why do you think Nancy is a good role model for young people today?

Applying What You've Learned

Imagine you have just been elected Speaker of the House. How would you handle this position?

Vocabulary

Elizabeth Cochrane Seaman (Nellie Bly)

journalism	anonymous	brutality	pseudonym
editorial	editor	asylum	rickshaw
suffrage	confer	corps de ballet	
outraged	slums		

Mary Jane Colter

visionary	integrity	geological	marketing
architects	archeological	strata	emulated
contemporary	plastered	hacienda	Great Depression
apprentice	phantoms	legacy	

Ka'iulani

heir	savages	injustice	guardian
prosperous	annex	mission	despair

Eleanor Roosevelt

humanitarian	diphtheria	paralyzed	injustice
mottoes	gala	migrant	delegation
press conference	politicians	sharecroppers	reform
instill	campaign	racial	polio

Georgia O'Keeffe

post-Impressionist	inspire	ordinary	critics
exhibit	unique	watercolor	still life

Dorothea Lange

immigrants	reputation	evacuation	Museum of Natural History
tenement	interfere	migrant	
polio	luxuries	retrospective	Guggenheim Fellowship
apprentice	drifter	Central Park	
stock market	longshoremen	Pearl Harbor	
Great Depression	sharecroppers	esophageal cancer	

Rachel Carson

conservationist	zoology	institute
chemical pesticides	ecology	chronicle
environment	topography	DDT
toxic	controversy	Academy Award
solitary	documentary	

Ella Fitzgerald

amateur	mentor	jazz	diabetes
reform school	Philharmonic	swing	amputated
encore	fine-tuned	scat	
bandleader	improvisation	imitate	
catering	rhythmic	quintuple bypass	

Rosalyn Sussman Yalow

enzymes	tracers	patented	inducted
insulin	twine	physicist	first-generation
diabetics	physics	aspirations	nuclear fission
radioscope	handicap	competence	

Nikki Giovanni

feisty	grant	eloquence
dean	festival	revolutionary
campus	anthologies	convocation

Donna Karan

fashion design	supersedes	ovation	launched
philosophy	boutique	wardrobe	reinvent
essential	misgivings	interchangeable	textile

Bonnie Blair

rink	technical	Olympic trials	consecutive
ceremonies	competition	meter	

Eileen Collins

gliders	chapel	simulator	debris
astronaut	credentials	disintegrated	tour of duty
scholarship	rendezvous	atmosphere	Mission Control
AROTC	vibration	maneuver	

Ruth Bader Ginsburg

meningitis	Social Security	prejudice	dissenting
Law Review	discrimination	policy	dean
constitutional	demoted	committed	ACLU
scholarship	diagnosed	gender equity	

Susan Butcher

musher	grit	blaze	leukemia
prestigious	remote	tundra	chemotherapy
unchartered	ordeal	layover	bone marrow
terrain	endure	harnessed	transplant

Nancy Pelosi

Congress	swearing-in	candidate	divisive
Speaker of the House	occasion	ballot	Democrats
podium	campaign	minority whip	Republicans
heritage	intern	majority	Catholic
political	neglected	mindful	minority leader
	volunteered	inspiration	

Answer Key

Elizabeth Cochrane Seaman (Nellie Bly)

Remembering the Facts

1. Elizabeth Cochrane Seaman

2. a popular song

3. to become a teacher

4. the *Pittsburgh Dispatch*

5. Any three of the following: women's suffrage; poor working conditions; problems working women faced; slums; divorce; the rich and poor in Mexico; Mexican politics; mistreatment of the mentally ill; her trip around the world

6. She acted insane so she would be admitted into an asylum.

7. her trip around the world

8. wrote about the problems that led to World War I

Understanding the Story

9. Answers will vary.

10. Yes. Nellie exposed many problems through her writing, and once they were brought to light, people often tried to do something to improve the situation.

Getting the Main Idea

She was not afraid to speak the truth, especially if exposing the truth could lead to reform.

Applying What You've Learned

Students might list ways in which they would draw attention to certain intolerable conditions to effect change.

Mary Jane Colter

Remembering the Facts

1. Pennsylvania, Texas, Colorado, and Minnesota

2. She said she would learn valuable skills that would help her earn money to help support her mother and her sister.

3. She worked as an apprentice to an architect.

4. She got a job teaching drawing.

5. Fred Harvey was building an empire of hotels and restaurants throughout the American West.

6. He hired her to decorate an "Indian Building" he had constructed next to one of his new hotels in Albuquerque, New Mexico. He was so happy with her work that they worked together for the next 46 years.

7. the Grand Canyon

8. She made up stories about them.

Understanding the Story

9. Mary loved the West, and if Fred Harvey was building new hotels and restaurants there, she wanted to design them so they would be as much a part of the land as possible.

10. Mary was concerned that any new buildings be as archeologically and culturally accurate as she could make them.

Getting the Main Idea

Mary refused to compromise. She has left us with realistic representations of the ways in which ancient Americans lived.

Applying What You've Learned

Mary honored the local landscape and culture by creating new structures that complemented the surroundings, rather than looking out of place.

Ka'iulani

Remembering the Facts

1. "the royal sacred one"

2. She explored her land. She enjoyed the giant turtles and the peacocks. She rode horses, surfed, and swam.

3. She went to school in England.

4. He eased her fears about going to England and convinced her that it was a good place.

5. She found out that the Americans were trying to take over Hawaii.

6. She contacted President Grover Cleveland and asked him to stop the Americans.

7. Her people were sad. Her gardens were overgrown with weeds.

8. She came down with a fever after being caught in a storm. Some believe it was the fever that killed her; others believe it was sadness.

Understanding the Story

9. She needed to be with her family and her people. Not only did they need her, but she needed them.

10. because the Americans did not respect the native Hawaiians

Getting the Main Idea

As young and inexperienced as she was, the Princess did all that she could on behalf of her people. It took great courage for her to meet with the President of the United States.

Applying What You've Learned

Answers will vary.

Eleanor Roosevelt

Remembering the Facts

1. They were wealthy New Yorkers. Her mother was not very kind.

2. She went to private school in England and was very happy there.

3. She had to return to New York City for her debut.

4. She volunteered in schools and joined a reform group. She examined working conditions in factories.

5. her uncle, President Theodore Roosevelt

6. She remembered how lonely her childhood was and didn't want her children to have the same experience.

7. She went where he needed to be. She kept the Roosevelt name in the public eye.

8. She traveled around the world to comfort American troops and work for peace.

Understanding the Story

9. No; she felt unloved by her mother, and both of her parents died when she was very young.

10. Eleanor was a compassionate human being. She saw a lot of human suffering, and she tried to correct injustice wherever she could.

Getting the Main Idea

Eleanor was loyal to her husband, and she was loyal to the American people. She was willing to take a stand (even if it was an unpopular one) to eliminate racial prejudice and social injustice.

Applying What You've Learned

Answers will vary.

Georgia O'Keeffe

Remembering the Facts

1. flowers, bones, clouds, and mountains

2. when she saw a watercolor of a red rose painted by her grandmother

3. her school principal

4. She felt held back by the style taught at the school.

5. She wanted to make sure none of her work looked like another artist's.

6. Anita showed them to Alfred Steiglitz who put them in his art gallery.

7. It was too crowded and noisy for her.

8. New Mexico

Understanding the Story

9. The principal of her school encouraged Georgia to paint whatever she wanted, instead of forcing her to do class assignments. She told her mother that Georgia should go to art school. Georgia's mother agreed and enrolled her at the Art Students League.

10. It brought her closer to nature—the flowers, bones, mountains, and clouds that she painted all her life.

Getting the Main Idea

Georgia had the courage to stick with what she wanted to do (be an artist) instead of doing what society thought women should do (be a teacher).

Applying What You've Learned

Students may explain how it takes a great deal of courage to go against others' expectations, to be who you want to be.

Dorothea Lange

Remembering the Facts

1. Her mother was a librarian there. Dorothea also went to school there.

2. She didn't fit in with the other immigrant children. She also walked with a limp.

3. Her father left home and didn't send any money.

4. Any three of the following: roamed the streets of New York: went to Central Park; went to the Museum of Natural History; went to plays and shows

5. She persuaded Arnold Genthe to hire her as an apprentice.

6. She followed a drifter to a bread line. She realized that life was in the streets.

7. Her photographs caught the attention of the government. This led to improvements in their lives.

8. She founded a photography magazine. She traveled the world taking photographs for *Life* magazine.

Understanding the Story

9. People fascinated Dorothea, and she photographed them to better understand their lives.

10. She used her photography as a means for social change.

Getting the Main Idea

Dorothea did not take popular or posed portraits. She took photos of the poor and underprivileged to persuade the government to better the living conditions for these people.

Applying What You've Learned

Answers will vary.

Rachel Carson

Remembering the Facts

1. a writer

2. She took a biology class and was fascinated by it.

3. her summers at the Marine Biological Laboratory

4. She was one of the first two women allowed to join the crew.

5. *Silent Spring*

6. the harmful effects pesticides such as DDT had on the environment

7. *Silent Spring* created controversy and awareness. Rachel went before Congress to ask for laws to protect the environment. President Kennedy read her book and put together a committee to investigate the use of pesticides.

8. *Silent Spring* strongly influenced Al Gore to campaign about environmental issues. Many of the environmental laws we have today are because of Rachel Carson.

Understanding the Story

9. Rachel loved the ocean; its plants and animals fascinated her.

10. She was against what pesticides do to the environment.

Getting the Main Idea

Rachel was not afraid to speak out when she felt an issue (no matter how big it might be) placed the world's environment at risk.

Applying What You've Learned

Answers will vary.

Ella Fitzgerald

Remembering the Facts

1. Ella's mother listened to the radio and collected records.

2. She moved in with her aunt and got in trouble with the law. Then she went to reform school, but ran away.

3. She entered a talent contest to dance, but she froze. She started singing when she couldn't make herself dance. The audience loved her voice.

4. Chick Webb

5. She was one of the first female bandleaders in history.

6. scat

7. She had quintuple bypass surgery on her heart.

8. Her doctors told her to stop performing, but she refused. Then she had to have her legs amputated.

Understanding the Story

9. Answers will vary.

10. It was their escape from problems in their lives.

Getting the Main Idea

Ella Fitzgerald is one of America's legends, yet she always remained humble, considerate, and supportive of others.

Applying What You've Learned

Answers will vary.

Rosalyn Sussman Yalow

Remembering the Facts

1. It is an annual award granted to the person who has done the most to benefit the world community.

2. for her development of RIA

3. Her mother's family was from Germany, and her father's was from the Ukraine.

4. Any two of the following: taught herself to read before kindergarten; loved math and was good at it; skipped several grades.

5. because she was a woman and a Jew

6. so she could take classes for free

7. They were trying to measure the amount of insulin in diabetics.

8. They could have patented the process.

Understanding the Story

9. She believed in what she was doing; she knew it could make a difference in extending people's lives.

10. Answers will vary.

Getting the Main Idea

Rosalyn refused to give up when doors to further education and research jobs were closed.

Applying What You've Learned

Answers will vary.

Nikki Giovanni

Remembering the Facts

1. She was unhappy at home. Her parents were fighting a lot.

2. She told her to read books by African-American authors and to write about what she read. Nikki learned that a writer could make a difference.

3. She didn't get along with the dean of women. She left campus without permission.

4. Her grandmother died.

5. She had to borrow money.

6. Her professors told her she couldn't write.

7. Any three of the following: cities, towns, churches, YMCAs, classrooms, bookstores

8. speak at the Virginia Tech convocation dedicated to the 33 students who were killed on campus

Understanding the Story

9. They had plenty of books and a piano in their house, and life was good.

10. her grandmother and her high school English teacher

Getting the Main Idea

She believes the best way to deal with racial prejudice is to celebrate that life that people are biased against; her philosophy is to build up rather than tear down.

Applying What You've Learned

Answers will vary.

Donna Karan

Remembering the Facts

1. Her mother was a model. Her father was a tailor.

2. She wasn't popular. Kids made fun of her. She didn't like her classes.

3. She lied about her age to get a summer job at a local clothing store.

4. Anne Klein

5. He owned a clothing boutique in Miami Beach.

6. Anne Klein had died, and Donna had to keep the business going.

7. She created seven essential pieces that all went together and didn't go out of style quickly.

8. She continues to work hard and "reinvents herself every season."

Understanding the Story

9. Donna's father was killed in a car accident when she was just three years old, and her mother had to work hard to support the family. Donna often felt abandoned by her mother.

10. Donna was a working woman, too, and she did not have hours to spend selecting clothes each day.

Getting the Main Idea

She designs clothes that make women feel good on the inside and on the outside. She helps them feel independent and self-confident.

Applying What You've Learned

Answers will vary.

Bonnie Blair

Remembering the Facts

1. Her father dropped her mother off at the hospital and went to the skating rink. Bonnie's birth was announced over the loudspeaker.

2. three

3. The town raised money so she could go.

4. She continued her studies and sent them by mail.

5. Bonnie won her first gold medal and set a world record.

6. five

7. She married a speed skater. She has been on the Board of Directors for U.S. Speed Skating. She has also served on Olympic committees. She wrote a book about her career.

8. She's a motivational speaker. She also does charity work.

Understanding the Story

9. She likes competing and skating as fast as she can.

10. She was highly encouraged by all the support.

Getting the Main Idea

She has the discipline to practice her skill and technique, and she races for her personal best—not necessarily always to win, but always to skate a good race.

Applying What You've Learned

Answers will vary.

Eileen Collins

Remembering the Facts

1. It is the soaring capital of America.

2. She read about it in books.

3. She worked in a pizza parlor.

4. It was the first year NASA allowed women to join the astronaut program.

5. He was also an Air Force pilot.

6. She had both flying skills and academic credentials.

7. She took out a pencil to see if it would really float.

8. She wanted to give others a chance to fly in space.

Understanding the Story

9. Answers will vary.

10. Eileen never thought she should get ahead just because she was a woman. She studied just as much and practiced just as long as any man in the space program.

Getting the Main Idea

She was not afraid to lead the way. And as a leader, she worked at building a team to achieve both her personal best and the best for her country.

Applying What You've Learned

Answers will vary.

Ruth Bader Ginsburg

Remembering the Facts

1. They encouraged her to work hard and told her that she deserved the same opportunities that boys had.

2. She was a baton twirler, a cellist, and editor of the school newspaper.

3. Her boss cut back her pay because she was pregnant.

4. be a teacher
5. Martin was diagnosed with testicular cancer.
6. She was a woman, she was Jewish, and she was a mother.
7. She wore baggy clothing so no one could tell she was pregnant.
8. Sandra Day O'Connor

Understanding the Story

9. Ruth became a strong advocate for equal rights and equal opportunities for women.
10. first from her parents, then from her husband and children

Getting the Main Idea

Ruth never got discouraged by all the gender and religious bias she experienced. She kept fighting to get what she wanted.

Applying What You've Learned

Answers will vary.

Susan Butcher

Remembering the Facts

1. when she bought her first dog
2. She moved into a cabin to learn how to live in the wilderness.
3. She and her team collided with a moose.
4. People said she cared too much about her dogs to win.
5. five
6. She learned she had cancer.
7. She was honored and glad to know that others would be helped, too.
8. She kept a journal for them to read after she died.

Understanding the Story

9. Susan was drawn by her love of country and animals.
10. Alaskans loved and respected Susan for her courage, her skills, and the way she treated her team of dogs.

Getting the Main Idea

Susan took meticulous care in preparing herself and her dogs for this grueling race. She raced as hard as she could, but she never forgot to appreciate the beauty of the wild country or the beauty of her dog team streaking along the trail.

Applying What You've Learned

Answers will vary.

Nancy Pelosi

Remembering the Facts

1. two
2. in the Little Italy neighborhood of Baltimore, Maryland
3. Her father was in the House of Representatives and later became the mayor of Baltimore. There was always political action in her home.
4. She got a job as an intern to a Maryland senator.
5. She moved to her husband's hometown of San Francisco.
6. She was elected to the House of Representatives from California's 8th Congressional District.
7. civil and human rights
8. 2007

Understanding the Story

9. One of the most important aspects of Nancy's childhood in politics was the many ways in which her father taught her about the need to help others and that "public service was a noble calling."
10. As a mother of five, Nancy has a natural voice of authority and experience in helping others get along.

Getting the Main Idea

Nancy is a strong leader who is also willing to listen to others who may have different opinions. Her background as a civil and human rights' activist is an indication that she will continue to work for the greater good as opposed to private interests.

Applying What You've Learned

Answers will vary.

Additional Activities

Elizabeth Cochrane Seaman (Nellie Bly)

1. Make a timeline of Nellie's 72-day journey around the world. Include a picture or description depicting each country or its people for the various points at which she stopped.

2. Research all the different kinds of transportation Nellie used (horse, car, train, boat, airplane, donkey cart, etc.), and write a short description explaining what it might be like to travel that way.

3. Make a poster advertising Nellie's journey.

4. Write a newspaper headline that might have appeared in one of the cities or towns through which she traveled.

5. Later in her career, Nellie wrote a great deal about social injustices. She would often go "undercover" to report on the problem as an eyewitness, as she did at the Women's Lunatic Asylum on Blackwell's Island. Do some online research to learn more about the history of the asylum, and to read some of Nellie's articles. Does the asylum still exist today?

6. Research Joseph Pulitzer, the famous newspaper publisher Nellie worked for. What is the journalism prize he created? Name some of the recipients and the work for which they were honored.

7. If you had only a single suitcase to carry everything you would need to travel around the world for 72 days, what would you bring with you?

Mary Jane Colter

1. Eleven of Mary Jane Colter's buildings are included on the National Historic Register. Read more about the register online at www.nps.gov/nr/. List five other buildings that you think should be included.

2. In the 19th and early 20th century, it was very unusual for a woman to be an architect and to receive such major assignments. Research other female architects working at this time. What buildings did they design? Were they similar in style to Mary Jane's?

3. Research Fred Harvey on the Internet. What did he do before he started to build his hotels on the railroad?

4. Divide into small groups to compare and contrast ancient Hopi and Navajo houses. Some groups should design a Hopi structure and others a Navajo structure. Are there enough natural materials in the environment today to replicate the original Native American constructions?

5. In 1916, President Woodrow Wilson signed a bill authorizing the National Park Service. Are there any unique areas that you think should be set aside as new national parks?

6. Make a map of the major cities situated along the Santa Fe Railroad in the early part of the 20th century.

Ka'iulani

1. Research the history of Hawaii's royal family on the Internet and write a short report on it.

2. Draw a map of Hawaii. Include all the islands and describe their geographic location in relation to the United States.

3. Learn more about the kind of ship Ka'iulani would have sailed on from Hawaii to San Francisco. How long was the voyage? Describe life onboard ship at that time.

4. What does it mean to annex another country? Why did the United States want to annex Hawaii? Which U.S. president was most in favor of this?

5. Draw a picture of Ka'iulani's home in Hawaii. Be sure to include all of the tropical flowers and vegetation, and even her beloved pet peacocks.

6. Create a timeline of Ka'iulani's life, including the people she met and the countries she visited.

Eleanor Roosevelt

1. Research the Roosevelts on the Internet to learn about the family's long tradition of contributions to American society.

2. Eleanor was a wealthy woman but she dedicated much of her time to helping the poor. Read more about her work with the Consumers League in New York City. Have most of the horrible working conditions she fought to change been eliminated in today's workplace?

3. At a time when a president's wife was supposed to quietly support her husband, Eleanor was often interviewed on the radio and also had her own newspaper column. She did not hesitate to voice her strong opinions. Brainstorm with the class to see if you can find other outspoken first ladies in U.S. history. If so, what were some of the causes they supported?

4. As independent as she was, Eleanor loved her husband Franklin. She always campaigned for him and often traveled to some of the poorest, war-torn regions of the world to speak on his behalf. How do you think Eleanor was able to balance being the wife of a public figure, a mother, and a successful spokesperson for human rights?

Georgia O'Keeffe

1. Paint a picture of a vase full of flowers. Then paint a flower growing outside; it can be in a garden, a wildflower in the grass, or even a weed growing in a crack in the sidewalk. Compare and contrast your paintings. Which do you prefer and why?

2. Alfred Stieglitz spent much of his life photographing Georgia. Look for some of his photos of her. Do you think he captured her originality? Do you see some similarities between his photos and her art?

3. Brainstorm with your class to try and determine if it would be easy or difficult for two such different artists to be married to one another. List the ways in which they might help each other in their work.

Dorothea Lange

1. Have each student in your class take a photograph of the same object. Compare and contrast the printed pictures.

2. Make a timeline of Dorothea's life, including where she lived and where she worked.

3. Talk with your classmates about some of the differences and/or similarities between painting and photography.

4. Dorothea used her camera to capture in pictures instead of words some great social injustices in the United States. Why did she think it was important to do this? Working in small groups, have the class tackle a current social problem. Ask one group to address the problem in writing, another to make a poster, and another to take a photograph. Have the class vote on which example was the most effective.

Rachel Carson

1. Watch the documentary *An Inconvenient Truth*, and then debate the points made in the movie.

2. Read *Silent Spring* and write a report on it. Do you agree with Rachel's position? Do you think the book is as persuasive today as it was in 1962? Why or why not?

3. Brainstorm with the class to determine if there are ways in which you can work to improve the environment in your community.

4. *Time Magazine* voted Rachel Carson one of the "Most Influential People of the Century." Use the Internet to learn more about some of *Time's* other influential people. Did any of the others dedicate their lives to protecting the environment?

Ella Fitzgerald

1. Bring an example of jazz music to class. Point out the ways in which it is different from classical music or from rock.

2. Jazz is spontaneous and improvisational. Paint an abstract picture that captures the spirit and movement of jazz.

3. Does anyone in your family have a special musical talent? How has this made a difference in your life?

4. Create your own song. If you cannot write both the music and the lyrics, try one and encourage a classmate to try the other.

5. Create a new album cover for one of your favorite singers.

Rosalyn Sussman Yalow

1. Read more about the Nobel Prize on the Internet at http://nobelprize.org/.

2. If you had a million dollars to create a prize, what would you award? How would you decide who the winner should be?

3. Rosalyn grew up in an immigrant community in New York City. What is an immigrant community? What do you think would be the most challenging thing for you to learn if you had to move to a new country? Brainstorm in small groups to discuss ways in which you might make it easier for an immigrant to feel like a part of your community.

4. Rosalyn was elected to the National Academy of Sciences in 1975. What is this academy?

5. Have you ever made an important or just plain exciting discovery by accident? Examples could come from formal or informal science. Share it with the class.

Nikki Giovanni

1. Read the text or watch the video of Nikki's Virginia Tech convocation address on the Internet. How would you define Nikki's ability to connect with people?

2. Divide into small groups and have each group select a Nikki Giovanni poem from a different era in her life. Read the poems aloud to the class and discuss the issues addressed in each.

3. Research SNCC (Student Nonviolent Coordinating Committee) on the Internet. When was it first created and why? Do you think it is necessary today? Why or why not?

4. Early in her career, Nikki received a grant from the Harlem Arts Council. What kinds of art did the council support?

5. Learn more about Nikki on her official web site at www.nikki-giovanni.com.

Donna Karan

1. Design ten interchangeable articles of clothing that would get you through a week of school in style.

2. Brainstorm ways that you might go about learning what styles were both comfortable and fashionable.

3. Ask the class what styles they like best, and compare and contrast them.

4. Do you think it's more important to keep your own identity or to keep up with changing fashion trends?

5. The Parsons School of Design is a famous art school. Research the other types of design courses they have in addition to fashion design.

6. Do you think it is possible to be a successful fashion designer without being a good businesswoman? If so, how could you make this work? Why do you think Donna Karan is so successful at both?

Bonnie Blair

1. Learn more about Bonnie and other Olympic champions online at the official United States Olympic Committee web site: www.usoc.org.

2. Look up the difference between a yard and a meter. Tell the class how many yards Bonnie skated in her 500-, 1,000-, and 1,500-meter Olympic races.

3. Find a stop watch or a watch with a second hand. As a group, time each other as you run 500 meters. How close are you to Bonnie's skating time of 38.99 seconds?

4. Make a poster of a world map. Mark the location where Bonnie was born, where she grew up, and the sites of all four of the Olympics in which Bonnie raced.

5. Research the other female skaters who competed in the 500-meter and 1,000-meter races in Bonnie's four Olympics. Note the countries they were from. Which skaters had scores that were closest to Bonnie's? How many competed in more than one Olympic games? Share your research with the class.

6. Brainstorm with a group to list some of the ways you might feel extra pressure if 60 of your friends and family had traveled a long distance to cheer for you in a race. Include things that might give you a boost, as well as those things that might be of concern to you.

Eileen Collins

1. Break into small groups to discuss whether or not you would like to be an astronaut.

2. Research NASA on the Internet. How many female astronauts are in the program today?

3. What is a test pilot? What kinds of planes are flight-tested today? How many test pilots are female? Research to learn if there are other means of transportation, such as cars, trains, boats, bikes, and so forth. that have to be test-driven before they are sold to the public.

4. Look up the National Women's Hall of Fame on the Internet at www.greatwomen.org/. List ten other women in the Hall of Fame and their accomplishments. Then report to the class.

Ruth Bader Ginsburg

1. Learn more about the U.S. Supreme Court at www.supremecourtus.gov/.

2. Ruth was one of nine women in a class of more than 500 at Harvard Law School. Who were some of the other women in her class, and what did they do with their law degrees?

3. Read more about Justice Felix Frankfurter. What were some of the most important cases that came before his court?

4. Ruth argued many cases on behalf of the ACLU (American Civil Liberties Union). Look up the ACLU and write a report to read in class. Be sure to include some of the many kinds of discrimination they fought to prevent. Ask the class to discuss whether or not the ACLU's work is important today.

5. Read more about gender equity. Do you believe it exists in America today? Ask the class to brainstorm about other countries where it clearly does not exist.

6. What is a "dissenting opinion?" Why do you think it is important to publish each of the nine Supreme Court justices' opinions once they have decided a case?

Susan Butcher

1. Susan Butcher was the second female musher to win the Iditarod. Who was the first?

2. Draw a map of the Iditarod trail and illustrate the different terrain on it.

3. Break into small groups. Each group should research a different Iditarod champion, and report to the class. After the group presentations, look for common characteristics shared by the winners. Describe any different strategies each winner may have used to win the race.

4. Research the Siberian Husky dog breed. What makes them so well qualified to run the Iditarod? Have any other breeds ever run the race?

5. What kinds of clothing would you need to wear for the race?

6. Research the tundra. How has it changed in the past 100 years?

Nancy Pelosi

1. Visit the U.S. Congress Votes Database http://projects.washingtonpost.com/congress/members/p000197/ to learn how Nancy Pelosi has voted on bills before the House of Representatives. Make a list of the ten bills most important to you. Would you have voted the same way as Nancy?

2. Visit Nancy Pelosi's official U.S. House of Representatives web site at www.house.gov/pelosi/. Click on the e-mail button and send her a brief note about something you would like to see Congress accomplish in 2008.

3. Nancy Pelosi represents the 8th Congressional District in California. How many other Congressional Districts are there in California? List three of the most important ways in which Nancy's district is different from the other California districts.

4. Nancy is the first woman to be Speaker of the House of Representatives. Do you think it is hard to be the "first" anything? Brainstorm with your class to better understand what things happened in Nancy's life to help her break this new ground.

5. Have you ever thought you would like to run for public office? Imagine you are running for a school election. Create a poster that outlines or depicts your strong points to help other students understand why you would be the best person for this position.

References

Elizabeth Cochrane Seaman (Nellie Bly)

Books

Christiansen, Bonnie. *The Daring Nellie Bly: America's Star Reporter.* New York: Knopf Books for Young Readers, 2003.

Ehrlich, Elizabeth. *Nellie Bly.* New York: Chelsea House, 1989.

Kendall, Martha E. *Nellie Bly: Reporter for the World.* Brookfield, CT: Millbrook, 1992.

Krensky, Stephen (Author), Rebecca Guay (Illustrator). *Nellie Bly: A Name to Be Reckoned With.* New York: Aladdin, 2003.

Kroeger, Brooke. *Nellie Bly: Daredevil, Reporter, Feminist.* New York: Times Books, 1994.

Marks, Jason. *Around the World in Seventy-Two Days: The Race Between Pulitzer's Nellie Bly and Cosmopolitan's Elizabeth Bisland.* Gemittarius, 1993.

Web sites

www.greatwomen.org/women.php?action=viewone&id=23

www.pbs.org/wgbh/amex/world/

www.americaslibrary.gov/cgi-bin/page.cgi/jb/progress/bly_1

Mary Jane Colter

Books

Berke, Arnold (Author), Alexander Vertikoff (Photographer). *Mary Colter: Architect of the Southwest.* New York: Princeton Architectural Press, 2002.

Grattan, Virginia L. *Mary Colter: Builder Upon the Red Earth.* Grand Canyon, Arizona: Grand Canyon Natural History Association, 1992.

Web sites

www.kaibab.org/gc/images/mjcolter.htm

http://search1.npr.org/opt/collections/torched/me/data_me/seg_114754.htm

http://search1.npr.org/opt/collections/torched/me/data_me/seg_114789.htm

http://tps.cr.nps.gov/nhl/detail.cfm?ResourceId=2019&ResourceType=District

www.myhero.com/

www.npr.org/programs/specials/architecture/0011.colter.html

www.npr.org/programs/specials/architecture/0011.colter.html

Ka'iulani

Books

Linnea, Sharon. *Princess Ka'Iulani: Hope of a Nation, Heart of a People.* Grand Rapids, MI: Eerdmans Books for Young Readers, 1999.

Stanley, Fay (author), Diane Stanley (Illustrator). *The Last Princess: The Story of Princess Ka'iulani of Hawaii.* New York: Harper Collins, 2001.

Webb, Nancy and Jean Francis Webb. *Kaiulani, Crown Princess of Hawaii.* Honolulu, HI: Mutual Publishing Company, 1999

White, Ellen Emerson. *The People's Princess, Hawaii, 1889 (The Royal Diaries).* New York: Scholastic, 2001.

Zambucka, Kristin. *Princess Ka'iulani: The Last Hope of Hawaii's Monarchy.* Kailua, HI: Mana, 1982.

Web sites

www.hawaiihistory.org

www.electricscotland.com/history/women/wh36.htm

www.aloha-hawaii.com/hawaii/princess+kaiulani/

www.longitudebooks.com/find/p/20338/mcms.html

http://kaiulani.freeservers.com/

Eleanor Roosevelt

Books

Cook, Blanche W. *Eleanor Roosevelt, Vol. I: 1884–1932.* New York: Viking, 1993.

Faber, Doris. *Eleanor Roosevelt: First Lady of the World.* New York: Viking, 1992.

Freedman, Russell. *Eleanor Roosevelt: A Life of Discovery.* New York: Clarion Books 1997.

Hershan, Stella K. *The Candles She Lit: The Legacy of Eleanor Roosevelt.* New York: Praeger, 1993.

Roosevelt, Eleanor. *The Autobiography of Eleanor Roosevelt.* Cambridge, MA: Da Capo Press, 2000.

Roosevelt, Eleanor, David Emblidge (Editor), Marcy Ross (Editor), Blanche Wiesen Cook (Introduction). *My Day: The Best of Eleanor Roosevelt's Acclaimed Newspaper Columns, 1936–1962.* Cambridge, MA: Da Capo Press, 2001.

Toor, Rachel. *Eleanor Roosevelt.* New York: Chelsea House, 1989.

Web sites

www.whitehouse.gov/history/firstladies/ar32.html

www.fdrlibrary.marist.edu/erbio.html

www.pbs.org/wgbh/amex/eleanor

www.time.com/time/time100/leaders/profile/eleanor.html

www.greatwomen.org/women.php?action=viewone&id=128

Georgia O'Keeffe
Books

Berry, Michael. *Georgia O'Keeffe*. New York: Chelsea House, 1988.

Bryant, Jen (Author), Bethanne Anderson (Illustrator). *Georgia's Bones*. Grand Rapids, MI: Eerdmans Books for Young Readers, 2005.

Buckley, Christopher. *Blossoms & Bones: On the Life and Work of Georgia O'Keeffe*. Nashville: Vanderbilt University Press, 1988.

Gherman, Beverly. *Georgia O'Keeffe: The "Wideness and Wonder" of Her World*. New York: Macmillan, 1986.

Kudlinski, Kathleen. *The Spirit Catchers: An Encounter with Georgia O'Keeffe*. New York: Watson-Guptill, 2005.

O'Keeffe, Georgia. *Georgia O'Keeffe: One Hundred Flowers*. New York: Knopf, 1989.

Rodriguez, Rachel Victoria (author), Julie Paschkis (Illustrator). *Through Georgia's Eyes*. New York: Henry Holt and Co., 2006.

Web sites

www.okeeffemuseum.org

www.artcyclopedia.com/artists/okeeffe_georgia.html

Dorothea Lange
Books

Cox, Christopher. *Dorothea Lange*. New York: *Aperture*, 1987.

Lange, Dorothea (Author), Linda Gordon (Editor), Gary Y. Okihiro (Editor). *Impounded: Dorothea Lange and the Censored Images of Japanese American Internment*. New York: W.W. Norton, 2006.

Meltzer, Milton. *Dorothea Lange: Life Through the Camera*. New York: Viking, 1986.

Ohrn, Karin B. *Dorothea Lange and the Documentary Tradition*. Baton Rouge, LA: Louisiana State University Press, 1980.

Turner, Robyn Montana. *Dorothea Lange*. Boston: Little, Brown, 1994.

Web sites

www.dorothea-lange.org/Resources/AboutLange.htm

www.masters-of-photography.com/L/lange/lange.html

Rachel Carson

Books

Erlich, Amy (Author), Wendell Minor (Illustrator). *Rachel: The Story of Rachel Carson.* San Diego, CA: Silver Whistle, 2003.

Harlan, Judith. *Rachel Carson: Sounding the Alarm.* New York: Macmillan, 1989.

Henrickson, John. *Rachel Carson: The Environmental Movement.* Brookfield, CT: Millbrook Press, 1991.

Kudlinski, Kathleen. *Rachel Carson: Pioneer of Ecology.* New York: Viking, 1988.

Lear, Linda. *Rachel Carson: Witness for Nature.* New York: Owl Books, 1998.

Locker, Thomas (Author), Joseph Bruchac (Author). *Rachel Carson: Preserving a Sense of Wonder.* Golden, CO: Fulcrum Publishing, 2004.

Wadsworth, Ginger. *Rachel Carson: Voice for the Earth.* Minneapolis: Lerner, 1991.

Web sites

www.rachelcarson.org

www.time.com/time/time100/scientist/profile/carson.html

www.ecotopia.org

www.rachelcarsonhomestead.org

www.pbs.org/wgbh/aso/databank/entries/btcars.html

www.greatwomen.org/women.php?action=viewone&id=34

Ella Fitzgerald

Books

Fitzgerald, Ella (Author), Ora Eitan (Illustrator). *A Tisket, A Tasket.* New York: Philomel, 2003.

Kliment, Bud. *Ella Fitzgerald.* New York: Chelsea House, 1989.

Nicholson, Stuart. *Ella Fitzgerald: A Biography of the First Lady of Jazz.* New York: Routledge, 2004.

Pickney, Andrea Davis, and Brian Pickney. *Ella Fitzgerald: The Tale of a Vocal Virtuosa.* New York: Jump At The Sun, 2002.

Wyman, Carolyn. *Ella Fitzgerald: Jazz Singer Supreme.* New York: Watts, 1993.

Web sites

www.ellafitzgerald.com/

http://museum.media.org/ella/

www.pbs.org/wnet/americanmasters/database/fitzgerald_e.htm

www.vervemusicgroup.com/artist.aspx?aid=2685

www.loc.gov/loc/lcib/9708/ella.html

http://www.greatwomen.org/women.php?action=viewone&id=2

Rosalyn Sussman Yalow

Books

Dash, Joan. *The Triumph of Discovery: Women Scientists Who Won the Nobel Prize.* New York: Messner, 1991.

Gleasner, Diana C. *Breakthrough—Women in Science.* New York: Walker, 1983.

Lindop, Lauri. *Scientists and Doctors.* New York: Twenty-First Century Books, 1997.

Straus, Eugene. *Rosalyn Yalow, Nobel Laureate: her life and work in medicine.* Cambridge, MA: Perseus Books, 1999.

Web sites

www.mssm.edu

www.nobelprize.org

www.jewishvirtuallibrary.org

www.greatwomen.org

http://web.mit.edu/invent/iow/yalow.html

Nikki Giovanni

Books

Fowler, Virginia C. *Nikki Giovanni.* New York: Macmillan, 1992.

Fowler, Virginia C., ed. *Conversations with Nikki Giovanni.* Jackson, MS: University Press of Mississippi, 1992.

Giovanni, Nikki. *Acolytes: Poems by Nikki Giovanni.* New York: William Morrow, 2007.

Giovanni, Nikki. *The Collected Poetry of Nikki Giovanni: 1968–1998.* New York: Harper Perennial Modern Classics, 2007.

Giovanni, Nikki. *Truth Is on Its Way.* Audio CD, 1993.

Giovanni, Nikki. *On My Journey Now: Looking at African-American History Through the Spirituals.* Cambridge, MA: Candlewick, 2007.

Giovanni, Nikki (author), George Cephas Ford (Illustrator). *Ego-Tripping and Other Poems for Young People.* Chicago: Lawrence Hill Books (Revised edition), 1993.

Giovanni, Nikki (author), Bryan Collier (illustrator). *Rosa.* New York: Henry Holt and Co., 2005.

Giovanni, Nikki. *Gemini: An Extended Autobiographical Look at My First Twenty-Five Years of Being a Black Poet.* New York: Viking, 1976.

Giovanni, Nikki. *Knoxville, Tennessee.* New York: Scholastic Inc. 1994.

Web sites

http://nikki-giovanni.com/

http://scholar.lib.vt.edu/ejournals/VTMAG/v13n1/page10-12.html

www.math.buffalo.edu/~sww/poetry/giovanni_nikki2.html

www.poets.org/ngiov

www.black-collegian.com/african/painted-voices/nikki.shtml

Donna Karan
Books

Sischy, Ingrid. *Donna Karan.* New York: Universe/Vendome, 1998.

Tippins, Sherill. *Donna Karan.* Ada, OK: Garrett Educational Corp., 1991.

Web sites

www.biography.com/search/article.do?id=9360373

www.vogue.co.uk/whos_who/Donna_Karan/default.html

www.infomat.com/whoswho/donnakaran.html

Bonnie Blair
Books

Blair, Bonnie with Greg Brown; illustrations by Doug Keith. *A Winning Edge.* Texas: Taylor Publishing Co., 1996.

Breitenbucher, Cathy. *Bonnie Blair: Golden Streak.* New York: Lerner, 1994.

Daly, Wendy. *Bonnie Blair: Power on Ice.* New York: Random House Books for Young Readers, 1996.

Greenspan, Bud; Foreword by Juan Antonio Samaranch; Preface by Bonnie Blair. *Frozen in Time: the Greatest Moments at the Winter Olympics.* Los Angeles: General Publishing Group, 1997.

Italia, Bob. *Bonnie Blair: Reaching for the Stars.* Minneapolis: Abdo & Daughters, 1994.

Rambeck, Richard. *Bonnie Blair.* New York: Childs World, 1995.

Web sites

www.lecturenow.com/People/BonnieBlair.htm

http://espn.go.com/sportscentury/features/00014107.html

www.infoplease.com/spot/winter-olympics-blair.html

www.usoc.org

Eileen Collins

Books

Atkins, Jeannine (author). Dusan Petricic (artist). *Wings and Rockets: The Story of Women in Air and Space.* New York: Farrar, Straus and Giroux, 2003.

Cullen-DuPont, Kathryn (editor). *American Women Activists' Writings: An Anthology, 1637–2002.* New York: Cooper Square Press, 2002.

Holden, Henry M. *American Women of Flight: Pilots and Pioneers.* Berkeley Heights, NJ: Enslow Publishers, 2003.

Raum, Elizabeth. *Eileen Collins.* Portsmouth, NH: Heinemann, 2005.

Richie, Jason. *Spectacular Space Travelers.* Minneapolis, MN: Oliver Press, 2001.

Web sites

www.jsc.nasa.gov/Bios/htmlbios/collins.html

www.nasa.gov/vision/space/preparingtravel/eileen_collins_profile.html

http://womenshistory.about.com/od/collinseileen/Eileen_Collins_Space_Shuttle_Commander.htm

www.msnbc.msn.com/id/12578454/

Ruth Bader Ginsburg

Books

Bayer, Linda N. *Ruth Bader Ginsburg.* New York: Chelsea House Publishers, 2000.

Henry, Christopher E. *Ruth Bader Ginsburg.* New York: Watts, 1994.

Italia, Bob, *Ruth Bader Ginsburg.* Edina, MN: Abdo & Daughters, 1994.

Klebanow, Diana, Franklin L. Jonas. *People's Lawyers: Crusaders for Justice in American History.* Armonk, N.Y.: M.E. Sharpe, 2003.

Roberts, Jack L. *Ruth Bader Ginsburg: Supreme Court Justice.* Brookfield, CT: Millbrook, 1994.

Web sites

www.supremecourthistory.org/myweb/justice/ginsburg.htm

www.supremecourtus.gov/publicinfo/speeches/sp_02-07b-06.html

www.aclu.org/womensrights/gen/24412pub20060307.html

www.washingtonpost.com/wp-dyn/content/article/2007/01/27/AR2007012701065.html

www.jewishvirtuallibrary.org/jsource/biography/Ginsburg.html

www.law.cornell.edu/supct/justices/ginsburg.bio.html

16 **Extraordinary** American Women

Susan Butcher

Books

Dolan, Ellen M. *Susan Butcher and the Iditarod Trail*. New York: Walker & Company, 1996.

Kimmel, Elizabeth Cody. *Ladies First: 40 Daring American Women Who Were Second to None*. Washington, DC: National Geographic Society, 2006.

Wadsworth, Ginger. *Susan Butcher, Sled Dog Racer*. Minneapolis, MN: Lerner Publishing Group, 1994.

Web sites

www.susanbutcher.com/

www.iditarod.com/learn/susanbutcher.html

www.achievement.org/autodoc/page/but0bio-1

http://library.thinkquest.org/11313/Iditarod/susan.html

www.adn.com/news/alaska/ap_alaska/story/8045345p-7938332c.html

Nancy Pelosi

Books

Marcovitz, Hal. *Nancy Pelosi*. New York: Chelsea House Publications, 2004.

Web sites

www.house.gov/pelosi

http://ustimes.us/nancy_pelosi,_pride_of_baltimore.htm

www.msmagazine.com/radar/2007-01-16-friedman.asp

www.csmonitor.com/2006/1109/p01s02-uspo.html

www.time.com/time/magazine/ article/0,9171,1376213,00.html

www.cnn.com/2007/POLITICS/01/04/congress.rdp/index.html

www.cbsnews.com/stories/2006/ 10/20/60minutes/main2111089.shtm

www.gale.com/free_resources/whm/bio/pelosi_n.htm